# How They Lived in the Yorkshire Dales

# W.R. Mitchell

W.R. 'Bill' Mitchell joined the Dalesman magazine in 1949, starting a journalis career inspired by owner Harry Scott's adage 'put people before things.' He to over as editor from Scott in 1968, a position he held for eighteen years. As well editing Dalesman and its sister publication Cumbria, Bill had a prodigious out extending across over two hundred books, innumerable articles and countles lectures. His thirst for knowledge and a keen listening ear made him an expert many topics. He had the skill of putting often-reticent Dales folk at their ease, interviews reflecting a bygone age and remaining for posterity in the W.R. Mitchell Archive.

In 1996 Bill was awarded the MBE for his services to journalism in Yorkshire a Cumbria and received an honorary degree of Doctor of Letters from the univers of Bradford. In 2007 he was awarded a Golden Eagle Award from the Outdoo Writers' and Photographers' Guild which cited him as one of the founding fath of outdoor writing. Two years later he was voted 'Greatest Living Icon' for th Yorkshire Dales National Park in a poll to mark the 60th anniversary of the National Parks.

In 2010 he won the Lifetime Achievement Award at the Dalesman Rural Awa ceremony, receiving the award from another advocate of the countryside, John Craven. Bill's work for Dalesman over four decades is arguably the defining feature of an illustrious career.
Bill died in 2015, aged 87.

First published by
**Castleberg**



ISBN 978-1-7391641-2-6

This edition published by
**Kingfisher Productions** - 2022
Watershed Mill, Settle, North Yorkshire BD24 9LR
www.railwayvideo.com

Printed by - The Amadeus Press, Cleckheaton, West Yorkshire

# How They Lived in the Yorkshire Dales

by

W R Mitchell

*Hubberholme Church.*

CASTLEBERG
2001

To

THE HILL FARMER

A dying breed

**Cover Artist**

David Hoyle, who provided the cover picture and line drawings, trained at Keighley Art School and subsequently, having been awarded a scholarship, at Leeds College of Art.

His favourite medium is water-colour. His special interest is in painting the rural crafts and activities of his boyhood in Cowling.

# Contents



Cover illustration, featuring seasonal tasks in the dale-country, was painted by David Hoyle.
Photographs by the author or from the author's collection. The source of some pictures could not be detected. Information about them would be welcomed.

## A Dales Lament

*Rewmaticks plague, mi pet corn twinges,*
*Mi owd knees creak like rusty hinges*
*This brocken arm long knit gives pain,*
*Sitch signs i' Yorkshire portend rain,*
*It's bahn t' rain!*

**P.R.S.**

# Foreword

Picture the small-time Dales farmer of sixty and more years ago. He is about to go to the fell to scan his sheep. In the tight family circle he is known as "dad". His wife, who was born and bred on a neighbouring farm, and is preparing him some bacon sandwiches, which he will slip into a pocket of his raincoat, is "our mother". When she impedes him in the big, stone-flagged kitchen of the farmhouse, he says, affectionately: "Git thi fat lump out o' t'way, our mother." She smiles back. His three children had set off on the two-mile walk to school. They will call at one or two outbarns and fodder young cattle that will be turned out to graze in May. The youngest of them, aged five, will lodge in the village until Friday.

The farmer's workaday clothes consist of oddments of clothing that have seen better days. He has a jacket, waistcoat, a flannel shirt and baggy, well-darned trousers. A cap with a stiff neb will protect his head from the extremities of the weather. He is booted, uses a workday crook to steady him on rough ground and has a dog at heel. His horse is kept at the farm for heavy work. From the fellside, he looks back at the dale, which is beginning to green-up and contrasts with the tawny hills. His small farm is one of several which are linked by a grid-iron pattern of drystone walls. He can see a score or more diminutive outbarns.

Our old-time farmer spends much of the day on the fell, gap-walling or kenning sheep, his lunch consisting of sandwiches washed down by beck-watter. It is spring. The fell is alive with upland waders – with tewits, curlews and the snipe that dives in the thin air and, extending the stiffened outer feathers of its tail, creates a bleating sound. The sheep are back on their high grazings after lambing time. The lambs will become heafed, attached to specific areas, as though they drank in their love of them with mother's milk.

On market day, the farmer wears his best setting-off clothes, with tweedy jacket and trousers bought from old-established tailors in the market town and guaranteed to last a lifetime. There is a fashion for leather gaiters, brown or black, kept shiny with polish. It was suggested to a farmer seen wearing a black gaiter on one leg and a brown gaiter on the other that the combination was unusual. He replied: "My son's got a pair, just same." Not many of the hill farmers can afford to have a car. They walk, bus or bike. Then it's back to the farm, with its two-milkings-a-day routine. Muck from the midden has been spread by fork to rejuvenate "herby" meadows which have not known the plough for many years.

Now picture the Dales farmer of today. Clad in light, weatherproof clothes, he sits astride his quad, a four-wheeled, all-terrain vehicle. The dog rides pillion. He travels at speed on road, track or fell. In next-to-no time he is in a fell-top world of rocks, coarse grasses, mist and murk. He keeps in touch with the farmhouse using a mobile phone. He has no time to stand and stare. Modern economics mean he has to run to stand still.

With the high mobility provided by his quad, he is back home for lunch. His wife bustles in a well-appointed kitchen and, having been a town lass, dreams of living in a nice little bungalow in town. His daughter, with her own car, keeps in touch with her friends by e-mail and thinks nothing of commuting twenty miles to a job in town and rather more for social occasions. His schoolboy son is "bussed" to school and keeps in touch with the outer world by Internet.

Dales farm life evolved in isolation. The farmfolk made a heroic response to thin soils, excessive rainfall and a winter that seemed to last half the year. The vet Alf Wight, alias James Herriot, who first got to know the dale-country in 1940, told me: "You could not help but feel sorry for the women who had to work in the big, flagged, draughty kitchens. The farmer's wife who opened the door to you very often had an apron made of sacking. Sometimes she had clogs on her feet. The dalesmen were hardy fellows. I was in my twenties. I'd see a fellow in his 70s shovelling snow away in the teeth of a cutting wind. 'It's blowing a bit thin this morning,' he would say. He'd just have a jacket on and I'd been wearing a muffler and a heavy overcoat."

Hundreds of little farms were scattered along the fellsides. Some of them had short, sharp names, examples being Cam and Cosh. More expressive were Winterscales, Gunnerfleet, Foxup, Hud's House and Middle House. The strong religious convictions of an earlier age were reflected in farms named Paradise and Israel. They were all occupied at the edge of living memory but many farmhouses stand empty and forlorn. Beams show through shattered roofs like the ribs of a sheep after the crows have had their fill. In their nakedness, they look pitifully small – hardly big enough for an average family, much less the large family of Victorian and Edwardian times. Ring-ouzels nest in what was once a bedroom. Rushes have reclaimed the gardens. When it is windy, a gate swings untended on rusty hinges.

At the hamlet of Booze, above Arkengarthdale, where life was never easy, a farmer commented: "Living's aw reet. It's gitting a living 'at's main worry!" Dalesfolk did not venture much beyond their own parish. An old chap at Appersett, who had never seen the sea, was not worried because "they tell me it's nobbut watter." He reflected for a moment or two and added: "Come to think of it, not many people have seen Appersett."

During the long winter, the average farmhouse was home to a dozen eager draughts and the base of the front door, which was rarely open, had a permanent lagging of old carpeting. During a particularly cold snap, Jack Frost painted pictures on the windows of unheated bedrooms. Some farms lost sight of the sun for a week or so in mid-winter. Cosh, tucked away in a fold among hills, one and a-half miles from the last settlement in Littondale, was home to William Brown and his family. When the area was overblown with snow, and sheep had empty bellies, Farmer Brown gathered them, mounted his pony and drove them across the "tops" to the Ribble Valley, where farmers provided a month's grazing for a penny or two a sheep.

At the head of Baldersdale, one of the tributary valleys of the Tees, Hannah Hawkswell emerged from a Pennine blizzard to become an international celebrity. Her bleak, solitary life was reported on by a writer for *The Yorkshire Post* and subsequently made into a television film. Hannah used the few daylight hours of winter to tend her small herd of cattle, her livelihood depending on the sale of a few surplus animals. Hannah told walkers on the Pennine Way, which passed close to her farm: "In summer I live; in winter, I exist."

When I first explored the Dales, most of the farms were unconnected with the electricity grid. Darkness lay on the face of the earth except where there was a faint light from hurricane lamps. Having been invited to tea at Bordley, a cluster of farms I approached from Wharfedale, then followed Tommy Birtwistle, the farmer, into his shippon and watched him milk the house-cow by paraffin light. It was the last time I was to hear the rhythmic swish of milk against the side of a pail.

# PART ONE

# *Winter Into Spring*

*Spring was a little late in reaching the dalehead farms. When snowdrops – the "fair maids of February" – were flowering in the garden, a farmer with less than half his stock of hay worried about having enough to see his cattle through the starvation months to turning-out time. On bitterly cold days, a hired man who was discouraged from entering the house, except at meal-times and when it was time for bed, would sneak into the shippon and warm his hands on the backs of cows.*

*In the depth of winter, the snow squeaked. Sheep overblown by soft snow might be detected by the tell-tale, brown-rimmed holes through which they breathed. Farmers had long rods for probing the drifts. The daftest dog was said to be the best at locating hidden sheep which, in due course, might suck their own wool for moisture. When drifts altered the contours to the extent of isolating farmsteads, folk who were naturally self-reliant were sustained in their isolation by a store of provisions, including sacks of flour for making bread.*

*By Michaelmas Day (14th of February) the days were visibly lengthening. On the moor, though heather and grass were low in protein, sheep snuffled for moss-crop, the flower-bud of a sedge known erroneously as "cotton grass". March saw the return of lapwings, known as tewits after their call. Cock tewits, with their extra-long head crests, were dandies. A pair would fly side-by-side, with slow wing beats. When she had found a nesting place, he would display, giving an exuberant call, pwee-eee-weep, while tumbling in the air. His vigorous beating of tufty wings produced a deep and vibrant wup, wup, wup. The lapwing, like the farmer, had a plaintive voice and was inclined to stand and stare. Hill folk felt that t'back o' winter's brokken when they heard a curlew twart [call].*

*On a bright March day, the owner of an entire [uncastrated stallion], having groomed and be-ribboned it, proudly led it to where farmers had assembled with mares to be mated. This was also muck-spreading time, the disturbed muck having a pungent smell, one reason why the Dales farmer's favourite sweet was an off-setting mint. Dales weather was perverse. There might be an April blizzard or even a May frost. It would be May before the cattle were turned out to graze. A farmer who had used up his hay said: "There's nowt for them to eat but, outside, look at t'view they've getten."*

Thornton Rust, Wensleydale.

# COLD DAYS, DARK NIGHTS

A Dales farmhouse door was rarely locked. Will Wallbank told how a kinsman at Keasden Head "got up and found a strange chap sitting at the fireside." A tramp had entered the house, stoked up the fire and gone to sleep. Everyone was welcome. If someone called at Will's farm, he'd say: "Tomasin [his wife] will mak you summat to eat." Cases of dishonesty were so rare as to become part of local folklore. Uncle Jack, a "rough-looking fellow wi' a gurt beard", had some property stolen – and soon got it back!

Through the long winter, Jack lived by himself at a remote farmstead, attending to cattle at several outbarns and visiting the main family house two or three times a week to collect food. He rejoined the rest of the family in summer, leaving the other farmstead untended. No one thought to lock the door. One back-end, he returned to find all his pots and pans were missing. A neighbouring farmer asked him if he knew who had taken them. Jack replied: "I do now. T'only folk who knew about 'em was us and t'fella who took 'em. Thou must have been that fella." His neighbour "fetched" them back.

Before the Great War, a "floating" population of workers were considered to be better-off than tramps but not so well-off as regular men. Such a worker would stay at a farm for several months, sleeping rough in an outbuilding, until he was "a bit fed up" and "bad to deal wi". One man, when paid up, gravitated to a local pub, living in the stables and went "boozing, boozing, boozing" until "t'brass ran out". He then returned to the farm.

Some non-Methodist farmers were inclined to strike t'spree [go on a binge] and if this happened on market day, the farmer might get back home two or three days later, sober but with no money left. Dick Harrison, a cobbed [odd] fellow who was frequently drunk, went with several other young men to a pub several miles from home. On the way home, he "started to become poorly and t'others took it in turns to carry him. When they reached his home, he was set down. He jumped to his feet and said: 'Goodnight chaps'. He'd played a cruel trick on his pals."

In mid-winter, the sun rose, spun in the sky – and was gone, leaving the air tinglingly cold. If there was no moon, t'dale lantern's gone out! At t'edge o' dark, one of the women went through the ritual of lighting the paraffin lamps, using fuel delivered in four-gallon stone bottles. The most irksome job was attending to a lamp that suddenly guttered, blackening the glass. This invariably happened during meal-times. The wick had to be trimmed and the lamp glass cleaned before normal service was resumed.

Outdoors, work proceeded with the aid of a hissing storm lantern. A dale held pin-pricks of light. In upper Swaledale, the occupant of a cottage on Kisdon could see only one electric light and that was in the telephone kiosk at Keld. A farming family went to their beds by candlelight and slept on mattresses stuffed with down plucked from geese killed for the Christmas market and painstakingly cleaned. Nowt must go to waste.

Monday, wash-day, was a "nightmare"; it involved the fireside boiler, dolly-tub and mangle, the last two being usually kept in the kitchen. Blackened stalks of heather that remained after swiddening [burning the moor to encourage fresh heather growth] made useful kindling. A wise housewife introduced some carbolic soap to the water in the iron set-pot so that her farmer husband would not be tempted to use the water when preparing food for young stock. A housewife's hands were blistered from using common soda in the wash-water.

Clothes were boiled, put through three lots of water, with some "dolly blue" added, and when almost dry were "ironed" using a flat iron of the type heated at the kitchen fire. The base was customarily spat upon to assess its temperature before use. In wet or dismal weather, clothing was dried on a rack suspended from the ceiling near the fire or placed on a winter-hedge [wooden self-standing rack]. A farmer's wife considered she had made a good job of washing and ironing if, at the end of the day, she was "played out".

A peat fire flavoured many a farmhouse. Coal was expensive stuff; you counted every cob you added to the fire. In any case, good peat warmed a "body" twice – yance when it was being cut and set up to dry on the moor in summer and yance when it was being burnt. One shortcoming was that it left a film of grey dust on everything in the room. The living kitchen being the driest room in the farmhouse, it was a good storage place for such as flour, which was poured into a bin that held some ten stones. Self-raising flour might be kept in a dresser, along with jam, also packets of sugar and coconut, a popular item early last century.

The fire burnt at its brightest in frosty weather. Some farmhouses had imposing inglenooks, complete with beehive oven and a spice-cupboard. The oven had been used for bread-making; the cupboard for keeping salt dry. Once a week, the ass-'oil [ash-hole, under the kitchen fire] was emptied, the ash being shovelled into a bucket for disposal. At a Swaledale farm, the hole was so large and its emptying so infrequent that, to collect it, the farmer backed a horse and cart up to the kitchen door. The dumped ash was soon being used as a scrattin'-place by hens.

A side-boiler and oven flanked the fire, the boiler being the major source of hot water. On bath night, a zinc bath placed before the fire was half-filled with water transferred from the boiler using a "ladin" can. Bathing was in order of age, the youngest first. A child brought from the bath, swaddled in a towel, sat on mother's knee and beheld a fire glowing with bright colours while mother used a tooth-comb to remove any nits [parasites] picked up from other children at school or play. On a winter evening, the fire would be built-up using a little coal and much peat. If the fire was overlaid with coal-slack late at night, glowing embers greeted the first person out of bed next morning.

The centrepiece of a living kitchen was a deal-topped table scrubbed as white as snow. Most farmhouses had flagged floors. Once a week, usually on a Friday, they were scrubbed with water to which common soda had been added so they would look well for the week-end. Where sand was not locally available, haytime workers were given the task of braying [hitting] pieces of sandstone with a hammer and storing the sand in a barrel.

Card games relieved the winter boredom. A group of men, meeting at a different farm each evening, played "nap" for 'awp'nys [halfpennies]. They supped home-made ale or gin. One of a group of eight, who became skint [moneyless], wandered into t'barn and lay down in t'hay. When he awoke, he found thruppence in his pocket, went back to the house and resumed playing cards. By morning, he'd "skint all t'others." Innocuous games like ludo and dominoes passed on the time between supper and bedtime.

Old folk kept their fingers nimble as they recycled unwanted clothes, deftly knotting the vari-coloured bits of fabric on a backing of hessian to create a pegged rug. The fabric they used had been clipped from clothes passed down, from one child to another, until they were threadbare, or from worn suits and dresses. The newest rug was laid on the kitchen hearth at week-ends. The oldest rug was a glorified draught-excluder at the back door.

Hand-knitting the old-way, with four needles and a dagger-like "stick" tucked under a leathern belt, kept the family stocked with gloves and socks. One needle was placed in a hole in the end of the "stick". The old-time knitters of the north-western dales, meeting in groups, had rocked and crooned as they worked. The songs they sang enabled them to keep a check on the number of stitches. Grannie, wearing iron-shod clogs, and sitting in a rocking chair, could be heard throughout the house.

It was the age of travelling tradesmen. A draper who toured widely used the train to his chosen area and then walked from farm to farm, measuring men for suits and trousers and selling bedding. He delivered as many orders as he could carry. In a remote area, a farmer's wife would augment the family income by selling a few groceries. "Kids could buy all sorts of sweets, including eight ribbons of black Spanish for a ha'penny." This housewife kept paraffin for sale in a lile building across the yard but refused to sell it after dark for fear of starting a fire.

The winter boredom was relieved by a stir [farmhouse dance]. Dancing took place on the flagged floor of the kitchen. The largest kitchens had room for sets of Lancers. A violinist provided the music. Where a pianist was enrolled, she would play until her fingers were raw. At a converted barn used as a village hall, a Mistress of Ceremonies, mindful of previous dances, announced: "We're bahn to hev no swinging the ladies off their feet. If it happens, I'll stop the band."

The band consisted of a pianist, drummer and two fiddlers, who occupied a corner of the single room where there was scarcely room to swing the proverbial cat. Three sisters were noted for being "as light as feathers" and adroit at dancing. The girls were formally asked to make up a "set" for the Lancers. They danced quietly away until they got to the last figure. Then one of the men shouted: "Now then – lift 'em!" They lifted the ladies high. The MC screamed: "Stop the Band!" so they shifted *her* off her feet.

People danced where they were not inclined to be leg-locked. The farm lads demanded value for their money. "If a dance did not go on till two o' clock, we wouldn't go to it." A man reared at a farm at the top-end of Wensleydale said it did not matter what time he got home as long as he was in t'house before his parents got out of bed. "I've seen me take my shoes off so my dad wouldn't hear me go to my room."

At a village hop in Craven, the wooden floor was so rough that a packet of Lux was scattered all over it to make it slippery. "During the dances, we were all sneezing our heads off." Harry Cockerill, who played the accordion at many dances, perfected his technique at High Greenfield, a remote farm near the source of the Wharfe. "I lived by missen for six years and being one and a-half miles from my nearest neighbour no one complained about my playing while I was practising." Transport from High Greenfield to the halls where he had been engaged to play was never easy. When he had a motor bike, he attached his accordion, in its case, to the machine using cow-bands.

After a cold snap, the onset of mist was regarded as a whiff of springtime. Carrion crows, garbed in undertaker-black, hung about the lambing crofts and dined on sheep afterbirth and on the eyes of any weak or ailing lambs that were left unattended. In spring a determined effort was made to reduce the mole population by trapping the wee beasties and flattening their slag-heaps. Moles were inedible but the pelts had a cash value for anyone with the patience to skin the wee creatures. "Tha needed a sharp pen-knife." The pelts might be nailed on a barn door with cawker nails [as used on clogs] to dry in the sunshine and breezes.

## CLEAN AND DECENT

The Dales farmer was mainly an outdoor man, milking cows, clipping sheep, draining, gap-walling, fettling anything that went wrong and making a regular visit to the auction mart. It needed a strong, native-born woman to run a Dales farm. Marry a lass out o' t'town and you married trouble. To the wife fell the mundane tasks of washing, cleaning, baking and butter-making. She combined such household chores with work out-of-doors, hand-feeding orphan lambs, helping to stack peat-turves on the moor, raking swathes in the hayfield (and nipping to the house to prepare the hayfield meal known as "drinkings"). She made black puddings at pig-killing time and acquired raw fingers when plucking the Christmas geese. In amonghands, she raised children.

A farmer who prided himself on his chimney-cleaning technique did not follow the unfeeling practice of using a fluttering hen. He tied some bits of holly together, then fastened them to a cart rope and a weight. His wife, standing by the fireplace, pulled the holly down. The routine was repeated several times and, to make "a reight good job of it", the inside of the chimney-pot was scraped with a dinner-knife. The flues of the kitchen range were cleaned-out using a cowl [coal] rake or the wing from the aforementioned geese that had been stored with others against such an eventuality. Displaced soot was bagged and stored against the time it was needed in the garden. The onion fly couldn't abide soot. "One year we got t'fly afore we had time to put on some soot. It played shell wi' 'em."

Drinking water might be taken from a spring or even a beck. Soft water, which had fallen as rain and was caught in a large system connected with the guttering of the house roof was ideal for washing because it did not require too much soap to lather. Many a cistern was composed of slabs of blue-grey flags from Helwith Bridge, in North Ribblesdale. The pieces were slotted into grooves on the base and also into each other, red or white lead being applied to the joints, which was why "soft" water was not for drinking. The protruding ends of the cistern were clamped together using iron bars and bolts, provided by the local blacksmith. .

A Victorian farmhouse might have three taps – hot, cold and soft – in the kitchen but in most farmhouses the hot water was drawn from a side-boiler in the kitchen range. A slopstone [sink] was of stone. Flagstone, invariably known

HOYLE 91.

as slate, was ideal where available, being impervious to water and therefore easy to keep clean. One of the minor uses for water was as a natural form of hair-dressing when the farmer's son was about to set off courting. He who anointed his quiff [hair on his forehead] was said to be "cawf [calf] licked."

On Monday, wash-day, the first task was to light a fire under the set-pot in the outer kitchen. The "kindling" might be pieces of charred heather stalks left collected after the latest moor-burn. The clothes, having been boiled, were put through several lots o' water and vigorously scrubbed. Dolly-blue was added to enhance the whites. Mother aimed to dry and iron the clothes on the same day. If she was not whacked by bedtime, she thought she had skimped the job.

The pantry, the coldest room in the house, was well suited for keeping foodstuffs and the home-made butter, most of which was sold to a dealer in the market town. Lying on the benks [shelves] were such items as perishable food, empty stone jars awaiting jam-making, new-laid eggs and, most conspicuously, shallow trays with sloping sides. Known as leads, because originally such items were made of lead, these trays were used in the butter-making process and might also be employed when salting down pig-meat. To make butter, milk was poured into the leads and left until the cream had separated, adhering to the sides. A plug was withdrawn. The "blue" milk that remained was drained off. Then the cream was scraped off and stored in a crock to await churning-day.

The larger farmhouse had a parlour or sitting-room, its wooden floor covered by coconut matting. A mirror hung over the small fireplace. The mantelpiece was adorned by a matching pair of pot dogs. The papered walls of the room held portraits of grandparents – "owd-stagers they were". At a house in Baldersdale, two portraits, similarly framed, were said to be of the grandparents. The stern-looking lady was grannie but the military person was no relation to the family.

"Mother said he looked like granddad, so we kept it."

If the farmhouse had three bedrooms, mother, father and the latest child would sleep in one room and the boys and girls have separate dormitories. In constricted accommodation, children went to bed in the parental room until they were seven or eight years of age. "There was a cradle – always a cradle for the latest baby." A number of small children might be arranged top-to-tail [head to foot]. To a child, brought up in a house with a four-poster bed, it was "scary" to occupy it with the curtains drawn. "It was like being in a bogey-hole." This bed had "frills all round – and such a weight of bedspreads [quilts]!"

In winter, little time was lost in undressing and donning night-attire. The bedroom was draughty, unheated and the ground covered with oilcloth. There might be a pegged rug by the bed to take the chill off the feet. The mattress would be home-made from calico bought from a travelling haberdasher and (as mentioned) was stuffed with the down of geese killed in the run-up to Christmas.

A prized bed-warmer was a brass pan with a lid, attached to a long pole. Being quite attractive, it was hung on the living room wall until required. When hot, but not smoking, ashes were placed in the pan and it was moved between the bedclothes to take the chill off the sheets. An alternative was a stone bottle that was filled with hot water. Left in bed, it was usually kicked to one side and, if it fell on to the floor, raised all the echoes in the house.

Furnishings in the guest bedroom included a bedside table made of bamboo. On the table stood a candlestick and, perhaps, a copy of *The Bible*. Elsewhere, a marble-topped table held a bowl in which reposed a jug of cold water needed for ablutions. A Wensleydale man visiting London for the first time stayed in a posh hotel. A member of the night staff saw him wandering about at six o'clock and was told by the dalesman he was looking for the kitchen. He always got up at that time and he always went to the kitchen for a wash.

The staff member mentioned that in his room was a jug of water in a bowl. He could have a wash there. The dalesman said: "Nay, lad – I've supped that."

A small farmhouse had little more than a stone-flagged living kitchen and adjacent pantry. The larger house had both living and back kitchens. Cleanliness came next to godliness. Several times a week, mother – in her working garb of blouse and skirt and hessian pinafore – filled a bucket with warm water. Then, with scrubbing brush and soft soap, she attacked "the green stuff" on the flagstones, cautioning everyone within hearing, on pain of a good telling-off, to keep off the flags until they had dried. At other times, a drop of milk in water, applied by cloth, gave the flagstones a sheen. The ceiling was lime-washed. Cob-lime was "slacked" in water, sometimes in the ground and at other times in a big boiler so the lime retained its whiteness. The walls might be colour-washed in green or pink. "When they got to papering 'em, it cost threepence a roll."

Economy was the watchword. A farmer's wife took pride in patching clothes, one woman being heard to say of her husband's waistcoat: "I've patched it and patched it that many times, I don't know which is maistest petch [largest patch]." Thomas Ayrton, who wore fustian trousers, sat a lot "and wore t'backside out." Not over-keen to replace the trousers, he had them "back-sided" seven times and "front-sided" seven times, using pieces of new fustian – a rough-and-ready job.

Women who in earlier life had been dress-makers were adroit with needle and thread. They had grim tales to tell of working conditions. One girl worked for a dress-maker from the age of fourteen to twenty-one. Her family paid for the tuition and also the cost of transport into town and lodging expenses during the week. This young lady was allowed to go home on Saturday lunch-time until early on Monday morning. After her period of apprenticeship, she had the status of an "improver" and received 5s a week.

# SUMMAT TO EAT

A kitchen's furnishings would include one or two wooden chairs and at least one rocking chair. "The boss would generally have a rocking chair." Children stood at the table for meals until they were too tall to reach the food in comfort. In one family, no less than seven children were chairless. A Wharfedale farmer started every day by drinking a bowl of fat. Another liked his bacon so fatty that he was dribbling from either end of his mouth.

Farmhouse cooking was "all ways" [ranging from good to bad] and generally plain. Farms with a poor reputation for catering were well-known to men looking for farm work. Someone might remark of a certain farm: "If you go theer, you'll get nowt to eat." With little spare cash, farmfolk lived austerely. The grocer made his round of the farms with white sacks of oatmeal, each containing ten-stone. This was served as porridge for breakfast and, in some farms, for supper.

Porridge was made in an iron pan on an open fire, being stirred with a wooden stick known as a thible till it was as thick as plaster, then doused with skimmed milk. Porridge "fills thi stomack and as everyone knaws, it's thi stomack 'at holds thi back up!" Dad might make himself some porridge when he came in from milking the cows. He had his own little brass pan that he presented to the fire. Another farmer took half a basinful of fairly stiff porridge and, putting a basin over his soup plate, turned the porridge out – just like a blancmange. It was shiny on the top. He then made a hole in the middle, into which he put a spoonful of syrup. Milk formed a moat.

Before the children went to school, mother doled out porridge and "when you'd had thi porridge you supped thi tea out o' t'same basin." The same practice occurred during the main meal of the day. "Thou had thi taties an' meat an' stuff on a plate. And then mother would put thi rice or semolina pudding on t'same plate." As the pudding spread to the side of the plate, a brown ring was visible. "The pudding had shoved what were left o' t'gravy to t'outside."

Oatmeal, when "thrown" on to a backstone to be lightly cooked, became riddle-bread. During the drying process, when it dangled from a rack or on strings stretched across the kitchen, it resembled wash-leathers. "As it got dried, you pulled it down and ate it. It was good when eaten soft but mother considered this was extravagant. It had to harden up." The riddle-bread not immediately needed was stored in a basket, covered by a white cloth, and kept in an airy cupboard. "It was served at the table in a lile basket along with a slab of butter. June butter was the tastiest."

Riddle-bread made a grand supper for a family whose appetite had been sharpened by clean air and hard work. A Keasden farmer had an auntie who was anaemic. "The doctor said her blood was nearly dried up – what was she eating? It turned out she was always nibbling at oatcake. It'd dried her inside up." Old Herb Tennant, of Newby, sold clapbread and riddle-bread from a horse and trap. "He struck t'spree [became drunk] one day. He got to his feet and paddled about in a lot of clapbread he had not sold. He called at Peter Green's, Chapel House. Peter cleared it out for him and gave it to the pigs.

Most of the food was home-reared or home-produced. In the garden were rows of taties and the ubiquitous patch of rhubarb. One patch was so large that a farm man, sick at having rhubarb as a "pudding" at every meal, took his scythe and felled the lot. The farmer's wife, not the least put out by his impetuous act, insisted that he tied the felled sticks of rhubarb into bundles and every stick of rhubarb was served (with custard) in the coming weeks.

A farm man who was weary of rabbit served up in various guises said: "What I could do with is a ferret." Snaring the humble bunny and selling it to dealers from town contributed to the family exchequer and in some cases paid t'rent. At a fellside farm that was "wick wi' rabbits", a man was employed to snare them. In twelve months he accounted for nine hundred. The brown hare of the pastures was less welcome than a rabbit; it tended to be a bit "stringy" and, to quote a farmer's son, "didn't keep so well – it was best roasted, straight off."

Farming folk did not buy much. Where the family and regular men were augmented by "knockabouts", mutton was often on the menu. They "butched" two or three sheep a week, the year round, simply sticking an animal in the neck and quickly reducing it to fore quarters, hind quarters, back and t'ribs. The brains, then regarded as a delicacy, were reserved for Grandad, who was t'boss. He ate them fried. The sheep's head, skinned and with well-scrubbed teeth, was then lowered into boiling water to produce a nourishing broth. Heart and liver were "relished". Mutton fat was spread on bread as a variant of bread-and-dripping; it was also useful for waterproofing boots. The fleece was collected by "t'potter-type folk".

Hens scuttered about the farmyard. Wooden coops were made for the old hen and its chicks. Into the farmhouse larder went eggs, dressed cock chickens and eventually adult birds. Geese, reared from gosling stage, were provided with simple little shelters in which to nest. If this was at the edge of a meadow, the grass grew thick. Farm stock dare not wander within pecking distance of the gander. A Burtersett family kept a broody goose under the kitchen table, which was netted round the sides to prevent the bird from roaming. At mealtimes, it was hand-fed with scraps from the table.

A variation on the theme of food-conservation was a wooden beef-loft, set in the kitchen roof and extending into the bedroom above. Access to the smaller type of loft was gained by lifting a wooden lid to reveal the hooks on which meat was hung. Such an arrangement was economical on kitchen space. (The bedroom was popular, especially in winter, from the rising warmth that took the chill off the air).

On baking day, a farmhouse wife made bread, teacakes, pasty and cakes. Fruit cake, rock buns, and scones were eaten with fresh butter. Variants on the pastry theme included jam, currant (with chopped mint), raisin, date and damson. Also on the farmhouse menu was Yorkshire parkin that stuck to your ribs and oatmeal parkin. Always there was parkin. If "comp'ny" was expected, our housewife would devote an entire day to baking. Precious china cups and saucers would be taken from the display cabinet. A silver teapot was brought out, together with a home-made tea cosy, which was brightly patterned.

A woman who bought bread was considered "shiftless". She should make it herself, using a bowl that held two stone of flour and adding to the flour half a pound of yeast and a handful of salt. "We mixed it with milk and water and stood it on the hearth. That was enough to make twelve loaves and perhaps a cob of bread or two as well. Brown bread was unknown. We got a great idea and called it 'coarse bread'. I used to go down into the foddergang of the barn where we kept the rows of provin [provender] and got a basin half full of bran – proper bran. I'd take that back into the kitchen when the dough was rising, get two or three handfuls of white dough, pour some boiling water and a bit of lard on to this bran, and mix it in with the plain white dough. It made the most beautiful brown bread."

It was therefore a common sight to enter a Dales farm kitchen and see dough in greased tins arrayed before a roaring fire where the dough had been set to rise. If it was rising too fast, the farmer's wife put her fist into it and send it down. Then it had to rise again. It was vital to keep an eye on the bread at all stages. (An inattentive wife found her cats were lying on cushions of dough).

When the dough had risen, it was placed in the oven and

the door-catch used from time to time to "let out the steam" or the family would get soggy bread. As it must last a few days, some fat was added to slow the drying-out process. The finest bread was that which had been kneaded the longest.

A variation on the bread loaf was to take a lump of dough, add more fat, spread it with lard, then roll it until it was a big flat cake about an inch thick. Cooked in the oven, it became Oven Bottom Cake. "My mother made all our bread. T'oven had to be at the right heat. If thou let thi fire go a bit low, dough didn't rise. Most weeks, the bread was tasty; then there was one week when the temperature had not been right and it had risen into what looked like big round buns. Mother said she'd have to make some more. What should we do with the old bread? We had a lot o' hens, at a hut on t'low side, half a mile away. Me and mi brother went to feed t'hens, carrying hen-stuff i' buckets. We had our hands full, so we kicked the lumps o' bread as though they were footballs. Each lump was still in one piece when we got to t'hen hut."

Sunday dinner was distinguished by a roast, usually "a big lump of beef", which had to be cooked slowly so that it was tender. Yorkshire pudding was made from a mixture prepared a couple of hours before it was needed. When the meal was almost ready, the roast was put on a dish in front of the fire. The "browning" had been poured off ready to be used for making gravy. Into the tin went good beef dripping. The tin was placed in the oven until the fat was so hot it began to smoke. Just before the Yorkshire pudding mixture was poured into the dish, a drop of cold water from the tap was added and the mixture was beaten up rapidly. The dripping-tin was brought out of the oven and within a second or two the mixture had been poured into it. Then it was placed in the hot oven and left for half an hour. The Yorkshire pudding rose splendidly. It was served by itself as a starter to the meal.

In the course of the week, the once proud "roast" featured at several meals. What was left from Sunday dinnertime was brought out for supper and served in sandwiches. On Monday, meat was served cold with pickles or piccalilli, mashed potatoes and cabbage. On Tuesday, if anything was left, it was cut into inch cubes as "hash" and subsequently the remnants were chopped and minced up to form the base part of a meat and potato pie, which otherwise consisted of chopped onion, mashed potatoes and turnip, well-season, with dabs of butter. A large boiled pudding called Spotted Dick was popular, being made in a big iron pan and "boiled for hours". Sometimes the pudding mixture was rolled out, covered with syrup, rolled up, put in a cloth and boiled for another hour or two.

# CHARACTERS ALL

In the spring of 1896, James Swindlehurst "flit" with his family to a little moor-edge farm at Keasden, overlooking the Three Peaks Country. He had rented the farm for £38 a year. James began his move on May 12, the customary flitting-date. His last journey was undertaken with his wife, two daughters and a year-old son snuggling on top of the load. As a long, low building appeared through the evening murk, one of the girls asked: "Is this where the cows sleep, Mammy?" The reply was: "No, love. It's where *we're* going to live."

The Swindlehursts were tenants of Bracken Garth, one of the little farms extending along the side of a deep gill to where it petered out on the moor. Life was frugal in a bleak setting, yet there was pride in belonging. Like the hill sheep, which were "heafed", the local folk were not inclined to stray. They were tenants of Ingleborough Estate. The agent, Mr Bateman, a quiet sort of chap, was driven about the district in a horse-drawn trap by Harry Burns, who had the grand title of coachman.

Mr Bateman saw that the conditions of rental were observed. On Rent Days – the twenty-first day of December and Holy Thursday – James Swindlehurst donned his best setting-off suit and, with sovereigns jingling in his pocket, made his way to the estate office at Clapham. When the rent had been paid, he was offered food and drink. A neighbour who did not normally sup anything stronger than milk, hearing the drink was free, had a bottle to himself. He staggered into his home minus his false teeth. Several days later, they were found at the roadside, where he'd been sick.

Keasden was truly isolated but gossip spread almost with the speed of light. A lad, aged fifteen, walked two cows from an outlying farm to Giggleswick railway station. On his homeward way, he saw a tramp lying at the roadside. The tramp shouted: "Now, me lad! Does ta knaw t'King's deeard?" [Edward VII]. The lad shook his head, to be told: "Oh, he died this morning." When the Great War broke out in 1914, the farmer who commented that "it's nobbut a bit o' bluff. It'll be over in a few days" was shown to be sadly wrong.

The dale-country abounded with characters. One such, at Keasden, was Old Will Lund, not forgetting his billy-goat. Children ran off when they saw the goat for at a certain time of the year it stank. Will never married and died when he was seventy-seven. On the previous year, when he went to the hairdresser in Bentham, he remarked that his mother was busy shopping. On his death, his mother was heard to say: "Aye, he was always a delicate lad, was our Will. I nivver thowt I'd rear him." Old Gornall of Rantree, managed to combine being a farmer with the roles of grocer and butcher. He slaughtered frequently and one week killed eleven fat sheep and two pigs. He was selling legs o' mutton at thruppence a pound. He "butched" in a shed behind the house and put his meat on display in the sitting room, which was also the place where he stored the groceries.

Happy Jack (John Wallbank) was, indeed, a happy-go-lucky type. As soon as his eldest son was old enough to run the farm, he began to roam the country, pig-killing and castrating horses, calves and lambs. On a visit to Malham, he castrated sixteen horses. When nightfall came, Happy Jack liked nothing better than to play card games – for money, of course. Away he went on a Monday morning, intent on visiting farms on Rathmell side or even Malham. As he returned at the week-end, he would be spied at a range of half a mile by his wife, who had gone down the fields to meet him. She had a squeaky voice, with which "she didn't half thrash him". Unperturbed, Happy Jack set off on Monday morning, leaving the farm work to his wife and eldest son.

Henry Swindlehurst Metcalfe arrived in the area from Kirkby Stephen to be shepherd at Keasden Head. He married Sarah Taylor and they farmed Butterfield, a modest holding of two meadows and two pastures. It did at least have an attractive house with one curiosity – the main door was set in the gable end. One night, his wife went to bed, expecting him to follow, which he did not. He had suddenly died. Mrs Metcalfe continued to do the work. Groceries for the farm were left at the school and the three children – Lizzie, Dick and Sarah Ellen – had the arduous task of carrying them home. Someone said to Sarah Ellen that her father's death was a bad job. "Yes," she said, "but in future I'll not have groceries to carry for him."

William Gornall was effusive if it suited him. When the time for the evening milking arrived, he would say to his son: "Good-lad, Billy. Good-lad, Billy. Fetch us t'cows in. I'll buy thee a new suit, Billy." He went on like this for a while until Billy demanded to know when the suit would be bought. Silence followed. Benjamin John Disraeli Haythornthwaite married Bella Cornthwaite, who had £500, a figure that impressed her friends. When Ben started horse-dealing, he proudly showed Will Wallbank what he considered to be a good trotting-horse. But first, he slipped into the house for a gun. The two men walked to a point near the horse. Ben slipped two cartridges in his gun and fired. "By gum," a bystander reported, "yon hoss's tail went up in t'air and the animal went round that field at full gallop." Said Ben: "That's the way to show 'em."

## HILLS OF SHEEP

The hills reeked of sheep. It had been so since monastic times. The old type of sheep included "Scotch-bred", the progeny of black-faced ewes crossed with tups purchased north of the border. Then folk got "fed up" of Scotch sheep and stopped buying them. One farmer made a point of putting back some of the Scotch blood every five years or so. A local "crag sheep" had been improved and the Swaledale had begun its triumphant expansion throughout the North.

The small-time farmers almost lived with their sheep. As one of them remarked: "If owt 'appened to me, my wife could look after herself. But who'd look after t'sheep?" The sheep were "heafed". A hill farmer's patience was continually tested by sheep. "Go into a field to catch one and it'd be so damned awk'ard you'd finish up in t'bottom land and have to snig it back out. It's just part of another day's work, innit? I say: 'Let 'em mek their own minds up.' They usually know where they're supposed to be going."

No two sheep are alike. "When you get to know 'em, you'll notice little things – face markings, leg colouring, set o' t'horns. You'll even see differences in t'shape of t'black patch ahint [behind] t'horns. One chap said to me: 'How do you manage to tell one sheep from t'rest in a crowd?' I telled him: 'I reckon tha could tell thy wife from two hundred other women'." To count sheep, quickly and accurately, was a vital accomplishment. Each farmer had a variant of the main system. One man counted in twenties - one 20, two 20s, three 20s - on his thumbs and fingers. Another chap who counted in twenties kept the score by transferring a pebble from one pocket to another as the sheep passed before him. A new lad, told to count the sheep, returned to say: "There are either 343 or 344." Said the farmer: "That's all reight. There's only supposed to be 326."

The breeding stock on the moor was in the peak of condition. Heather being hard on their teeth, each autumn the older animals were drafted to the sales and from here to lowland farms where they were crossed with mutton-producing strains. Meanwhile, the hoggs [young sheep] were given a holiday on low ground, usually by the sea. Sheep left at home carried their lambs through the coldest, wettest, darkest months of the year to produce them as the weather ameliorated in April. The hoggs returned, to be incorporated in the flock.

Nothing suited a fell farmer more than to see his sheep spread out on the moor. A shepherd was hired on the stinted pastures, one of his jobs being to ensure that no part of the area was over-grazed. A Cowgill man who shepherded on Cam End was paid 18s.6d a week. He lodged at the home of one of the gamekeepers. His mother did the baking. He collected it on his weekly visit home. In many big, open areas, where there were outcropping rocks and bogs, the stint [representing the pasturage of a single sheep], was the basic unit of stocking. A number of stints was allocated to each of the local farms depending on size. At Ribblehead, the stint-holders met at Gearstones on the first Saturday in February to discuss mutual matters. Old Bob Staveley, mine host, kept them supplied with ale. Jock Carrick, a Scot who worked as the gamekeeper for the Ingleborough Estate, and therefore had a concern about the state of the moor, was usually present.

Sheep illnesses had been given curious names. In early spring, when sheep were heavy with lamb, dozens might go down with calcium deficiency, known variously as moss-illness, tremblings and staggers. In grandfather's days the cause being unknown, it could gravely cull a flock. "They gave 'em treacle. If one got better, that were t'cure. From then on, all t'sheep got treacle." On the western moors are the remains of shepherds' cabins at which those sheep troubled by "moss illness" were lambed. Each spring, one farmer released an old boar [pig] on to the fell to clean up the dead sheep. It is said to have lived on carcasses until early summer. Moss-illness, also known as braxy, might afflict some good hoggs in autumn. The farmer sighed when he found them lying with distended bodies and "a gurt lot o' froth around each nostril". The sheep had been healthy to the end. They died where they stood.

Another illness, attributed to strange dogs fouling the ground, was called "sturdy". An affected sheep began to walk in a circle. In days before vets were commonly used, a knowing farmer felt the skull for a soft spot and burnt through the bone with a hot metal rod. From the wound oozed "a lot of o' watery stuff", plus the parasites that caused the complaint, removed using a quill. An application of green salve to the wound bound it up. "I remember mi dad takkin' it out... Some sheep lived. And some sheep died." Bracken harboured sheep-ticks. A scientist who took away a tick for study found it subsequently laid about two thousand eggs from which 1,500 young ticks hatched. If ticks infected sheep they might get "louping illness."

Well-trained sheepdogs eased the effort of gathering sheep. A lile chocolate-coloured dog out of Quernmore that lived to be fourteen years old was a bit short in t'leg, keen to run but soon got tired in rough ling. A man who claimed to have the best dog in Mewith said: "I open t'window in a morning and shout. By t'time I've dressed and gone downstairs, t'dog has milk cows at t'gate. I've thowt many a time that if I only had sense to leave t'gate oppen, it would have 'em tied up."

Sheep were "gathered" for lambing, dipping, clipping and spaining [the separation of ewes from their lambs]. The farmer brought his sheep to lower ground if there was a blizzard in the offing.

Special marks distinguished one stock of sheep from another. A piece clipped out of an ear in a special position and a daub of a colourful fluid across the fleece confirmed the matter of ownership. To the Norsefolk of old, the ear-clip was a "law mark", which became "lug" – hence the fate of a naughty child to have his lug [ear] clattered. In the old days, tar was used as a marking fluid, to the annoyance of the wool merchants, for tar would not scour out at the textile mill.

A farmer felt half-dressed without his crook. He might have half a dozen crooks, one being for general work and another – a catching stick – coming into its own at lambing time. The shape of the crook wrapped itself comfortably around the neck of a lamb or a sheep that needed attention. A market-crook was for "setting off". The traditional crook was formed of tup horn, boiled to soften it so the curl might be varied. The best crook had a shaft of hazel or blackthorn.

The hill folk were weather-wise – up to a point. Two neighbours were working among the sheep in Maytime when a storm approached. They "nipped into t'farmhouse" for a drink of tea and, the storm being over, they returned to the sheep and to attend to cows in a shippon. The top part of the shippon door had been left open. Lighting had killed the first four cows. It would have been the fate of the two men if they had sheltered here instead of heading for home.

# LAMBING TIME

On a hill farm, when tupping time arrived, nature was allowed to take her course. If all the sheep did not lamb, it did not matter too much. On lower ground, where rents were highest and sheep dearer, it was vital that all the ewes produced offspring. "You had to be a bit more particular at tupping time." Heavily pregnant ewes were taken off the moor or common and quartered in crofts near the farmhouse, where they might be inspected several times a day and not often at night. "You couldn't disturb these sort o' sheep at night. If you walked among them, they'd run away. They were better left, under t'wall, sheltered from wind and wet." In 1917, when snow and frost continued well into the spring, a farmer and his daughter lambed sixty and reared nineteen of them. Twelve were reared on t'bottle and seven on sheep. The farmer said, grimly: "A ewe dropped its lambs, looked back at them, baa-ed twice – and left 'em."

In spring, it was surprising how well a lamb survived in grim conditions when it had been licked clean and provided with milk by its mother. Chilled lambs were given milk into which a hot poker had been plunged to raise the temperature and sterilise it. Other lambs were plunged into hot water or left in the fireside oven, with an open door, until they warmed up. Sometimes a chilled lamb was sunk up to its neck in a steaming horse-midden. There was nowt like a drop of brandy for a starved lamb. "One lamb was in such a poor way, we gave it some brandy, put the lamb in t'oven for a while. It went to sleep. There was never a movement for an hour or two. Then it started waking up and moving about. It was soon all right."

Orphan lambs were "a handful". A lamb that had been orphaned or had a mother who was short of milk was "fed a cow pap. You didn't use a bottle wi' a tit on." The farmer sat on a stool beside a thin-titted cow as if he intended to milk it. Instead, he had the lamb on his knees. "Then you'd 'od it's head up, nose up to t'cow tit and squirt milk into lamb's mouth. If tha were lucky, yon lamb would soon be sucking by itself."

One year, when this family had four pet lambs, they thrived and, aged two months, were unusually large. "It turned out that they'd been sucking cows. When it got into August, them cows wanted drying-off [at the end of the lactation]. We took 'em into t'low pasture out o' t'way. Father said one day: 'Hest ta sin owt o' them fower pet lambs?' I hadn't so I went into t'low field. Those four pet lambs were wi' t'cows. They'd gone back to their mothers, if you will. We had to fasten 'em in." One precocious lamb ventured into the yard where men were dipping sheep and was thrown into the smelly mixture. Everyone laughed at its plight. Laughter turned to annoyance when the lamb entered the farmhouse – and shook itself before the fire. Goats were kept to be used as mobile milk bars in bad weather. A farmer who kept a goat or two noted how they dropped their kids early in the year. There was a good milk flow by the time the sheep were lambing. On his rounds, a farmer might have a goat on a lead, milking it direct into the mouth of a needy lamb.

# OUTBARNS

Nowhere are outbarns seen in greater number and diversity than in upper Swaledale. You might take in a score or more at a single glance. In the heyday of the outbarns, the human population was large and the land split into quite small plots. A typical upland barn, of two-storey height, is rectangular in shape. Strictly speaking, it is more than a barn, having evolved for the over-wintering of young cattle, hence its siting near a spring. The "beeasts" were turned out daily to drink. In wild weather, they didn't want to go out and had to be driven.

Above the little shippon or "liggin" were "baulks" for storing hay. The main store of hay was known variously as "mewstead" or "moo". In Swaledale, a small barn might be referred to as a "field house" or, more commonly, coo'us [cowhouse]. Most barns were built on sloping ground, with a forking-hole on the top-side. Hay was fed directly into the topside from a sled or cart. On the low side, where the cattle were quartered, their dung was shovelled through a hole into a muck-midden and subsequently deposited from a cart into small heaps, from which, in early springtime, it was spread finely by hand-fork to revive local meadows. The Shorthorn cow, mainstay at the little farms, was a thrifty animal, unlike some breeds which "hed their heeads in t'barn and their arses ower t'midden."

Outbarns provided unofficial lodgings for the many tramps who wandered about the dale-country. Kindly folk provided them with meals. Sleeping in a barn was a chancy business. One tramp ran the risk of decapitation when a farmer, unaware of his presence, began to use a "mew spade" to cut hay – and, with seconds to spare, saw a man's arm appear above the top of the mew. In the heyday of the little farms, a hay-knife of immense size was used to cut into the mow for hay when the cattle were to be fed. It was hard, laborious work if the hay had been won in poor weather and had become claggy. The spores, inhaled by the farmers, led to a complaint that was later termed "farmer's lung".

It was likely that a farm man would visit the outbarns three times a day. He toured them "first thing" to feed stock, then in mid-morning he'd turn out the cows to water and meanwhile "muck out", dumping the dung in a handy midden. He would also get some hay ready for the evening feed. "It was usually dark when I went along then. I just shoved hay over to them."

Jim Metcalfe, aged fourteen, remembered Ryelands, at Arncliffe, as a happy farm though "wi' quite a few outbarns I had some running about to do. I nipped round the barns first thing in the day and then went back to the farm, picked up a back-can and biked to a barn a mile below the village where I milked cows by hand. By then, it was time for breakfast. I wasn't encouraged to sit for long for there was mucking-out to do." As related, lads on their way to school called at the outbarns to fodder the cattle. The devil had work for idle hands. It was not unusual for a ten-year-lad to be milking cows at home before he went to school and, on his return to the farm, to help with the milking before sitting down to a meal. "You had a three-legged stool. You sat down, gave a cow a bit o' provin, milked it while it ate, then went on to t'next."

A lad who did not make a satisfactory job of milking ended up with "more muck na milk." He ruefully explained that t'cow 'ud lifted its leg or swished its tail and a cob o' muck had gone into t'bucket. "At t'end o' t'day, milk went through a sort o' sieve, but nobody took any harm, did they?" If you could get a cow that was "well-drawn", milk came up t'bucket wi' a head on it as good as on a pint o' beer. Froth would go over t'bucket side, taking any muck with it.

# WALLS WITHOUT MORTAR

A visitor from town in extremely wet weather had to pick his way carefully over muddied areas at the approaches to gates. He asked the farmer: "Why do you always put the gateway in the muckiest part of the field?" Jossie Atkinson, a great waller in Mallerstang, had an aversion to standing on muddy ground as he worked. A waller like Jossie could, in his prime, wall a rood [seven yards in the dale-country] during a summer's day. It was the hallmark of a good waller that when he picked up a stone he had kenned [found] a place for it. A Dales waller of the old type worked by t'rack o' t'eye.

With a drystone wall, you've got bield [shelter] for the stock. When the weather was "howling cold" but dry, all the sheep were ligging on t'lee side of the wall. They had their bit o' bield. A hired man who thought he was being enterprising draped walls with damp hay instead of putting it in *foot-cocks* or *pikes*. No-one had time to bother with the hay on the walls. It just withered and blew away.

A drystone wall is really two walls in one, bound together with long stones called "throughs", packed with small stones and finished off with a row of capstones. The freeze-thaw conditions of a hard winter played havoc with weak stretches of a wall which, having been held firm by a prolonged frost, shifted with the thaw. If a fellside farmer had nowt else to do, he'd go and wall a gap. If there was a bad spot in a wall, he knocked it down and re-built it. Why cobble [fettle] it when you'd soon have t'job to do reight?

From the moment of its completion, the stones of a drystone wall are in a constant state of readjustment, being subject to changes in the land surface and to variations of warmth and cold. With the spring thaw, the south side of the wall warms up first, dispersing the snow. Frost remains on the other side of the wall or, in Dales talk, "back is still ice". Next thing you know, ten yard of wall have tummelled. It is an eerie experience to walk in the Dales on a still morning after a cold snap, when suddenly a considerable length of wall collapses with a clatter and cloud of dust.

Wall-ends, such as at gateways, were neatly finished and each field had a low gap known as a "cripple-hole", which permitted sheep to move from one pasture to another while restraining cattle. One hole was big enough to take a Shetland pony. When a child clambered on the back of the pony for fun, the animal made directly for the hole. The rider had to make a rapid escape. When a couple of aggressive Scotch tups met in the middle of a cripple-hole, "they didn't upset t'wall but by gow you could have heard t'crack of horn against horn in t'next parish."

The walls faithfully recorded the geology of each area for no-one was going to carry big stones far. They got them locally. Some stone used at Hazlewood and Storiths, in Wharfedale, was hard stuff, like granite and, at some time, had been "smoothed over wi' watter". A man who gap-walled for a farmer had "a heck of a job". The waller told him it was bad stuff to wall with. Said the farmer: "It looks as though t'damn pigs have been at it." The waller remarked: "If thou gets any pigs near this, it'll be down again."

# OUT O' T'BOTTLE

William Capstick, a blacksmith living at Clapham, was renowned for doctoring horses and was regularly called upon to pull out "wolf teeth", which formed behind the grinders and gave the animal difficulty in eating. He performed this operation using hammer and chisel and therefore had one chance. A wounded horses would not give him another. William was equally adroit at pulling bad teeth from local people. Big, strong and making the scales dip at eighteen stone, he would persuade a patient to lie on an old sofa. Once had had his knee on the visitor's chest, there was no escape. Pliers were used to yank out a troublesome molar. There was no anaesthetic. Local people tended to prefer an aching tooth, daubed with whisky, to Mr Capstick's dentistry.

A sheep was not ill for long. It would recover – or die. An owd yow that had been torn to bits while giving birth to its lambs was dosed with barbiturate by a vet who considered the best course was to put her out of her pain. A week later, the vet called to another lambing yow at the same farm. The farmer pointed at a grazing sheep and said that this was the one the vet had injected. Instead of dying, the sheep had slept for three days and then got up and wanted a bit of hay. She started eating again. Irvings, of Skipton, made up a powder, in a paper packet, that was supposed to cure a form of dysentery that was killing thousands of young lambs. The powder was poured into a bottle of milk and fed to the lamb. Another powder, mixed with a little gin, fortified any ailing lambs.

The vet was a member of a macho-profession. He stripped to the waist, summer and winter, for almost every task. He spent an inordinate amount of time with his arms up bovine orifices. As Donald Sinclair used to say: "There's a whole lot to be learnt up a cow's backside." When there were no plastic gloves, vets suffered from brucellosis and, consequently, a depressive illness known as undulant fever.

The vet, like a doctor, was an expensive luxury to a hill farmer whose profit and loss account was roughly in balance. Every farmer had his remedies for the many sheep ailments. Lambs that had diarrhoea were dosed with castor oil. A farmer who was feeling off-colour might swig medicine that was intended for livestock. He went through the time-honoured practice of shaking the bottle before use.

Alf Wight, who would become world-famous as a writer under his pseudonym James Herriot, assisted a vet called Frank Bingham, an Irishman, based at Leyburn in Wensleydale. Frank was a charming, laid-back man who didn't care. Yet he could cast a wild colt with one hand while rolling a cigarette with the other. In common with a lot of vets at the time, Frank was virtually an alcoholic. Get him into the *Wensleydale Heifer* at West Witton, the *CB* in Arkengarthdale or one of several pubs at Leyburn and he was immovable. A farmer who sent for him might have to wait for days before he "landed up".

## PART TWO

# *Spring Into Summer*

*This was the bonniest time of the Dales year, except for the housewife. The strengthening sunshine had shown up the dust and cobwebs in the house. Spring-cleaning was at hand. Everything washable must be washed. Carpets were beaten and goose-wings used to remove cobwebs from behind large pieces of furniture.*

*With the sheep and lambs up the hill, the gates of the meadows were kept closed so that the grass might grow unhindered by grazing animals. Curlews dipped and called. In the fellside gills, cock ring ouzels roused the echoes with their clear piping song or harsh alarm call – tac, tac, tac. Thorn trees stood with arms full of white or red blossom. This was known as "May blossom" though its full effect would not be seen until early June.*

*On turning-out day, in May, the cows emerged from winter cover, their bodies matted with dung. The dewy grassland cleansed them and a change of diet, from hay to grass, was detectable in the improved quality of the milk. Twice a day the cows returned to the shippons to be milked. On some hill farms, milking was an outdoor event. A farmer kept the three-legged stool on a wall-top or in the outbarn. He transported the milk to the farm by back-can.*

*At remote Cosh, beyond Littondale, up to fifty cattle belonging to other farmers were gisted [summered]. Among them were Scottish beasts, bought by the Pratts of upper Wensleydale so they might be fattened up on the rich Craven grazings.*

*On the moor, hen grouse, which sat so tightly on their nests they were like feathered tea-cosies, now led broods of chicks through a mini-jungle of heather to the boggy places where insects and grubs abounded. The precocious chicks would soon be trying out their stubby wings.*

# TIME FOR PRAYER

Spring was a time for spiritual spring-cleaning. At Easter, a succession of services led the dalesfolk through the most doleful, then the most joyous days in the Christian calendar. Most people went to church. Others "nivver darkened t'doorstep of a place o' worship 'cept to be baptised, wed and buried." Someone asked a hill farmer's wife if she knew that one of her lads had been going to church on Sunday afternoon. She said: "It maks no odds where he goes as long as he dresses up and goes somewhere. I'm not having 'im loitering about here." She had her own moral code. When her youngest sons began to visit friends at a neighbouring farm on Sundays, mother was keen to know if they had been on their best behaviour, adding: "If they haven't – I'll straiten 'em!"

On Sunday, a deafening hush descended on the dale-country. You could hear the wax crackling in your ears. The air quivered with a murmuration of insects. No unnecessary work was done. Pious families wended their way along farm tracks and roadway, each family sitting in a pew used by their forebears and singing well-remembered hymns. The men wore suits of crow-black, the women having sensible but patterned dresses – a neat reversal of the situation in nature where the male was usually the brightest of the pair.

At old churches like Hubberholme, in Wharfedale, the air of mystery was heightened by the limited daylight and castellated tower. Who would give a second glance at a chapel, which usually was plain, with the proportions of a shoebox, a steeply-sloping roof and a porch stuck on as though it was an afterthought? The little Methodist chapel at Castle Bolton started out life as two cottages. The farmstead known as Miil Dam, above Bentham, was used for Sunday services. Forms stacked in the barn were brought into the parlour and the rostrum was slipped over the back of an ordinary chair for the use of the preacher who, if he let his mind wander for an instance, would notice that the window framed a glorious view of Ingleborough.

Dales chapels were as austere and unpretentious as the dalesfolk themselves. In the smallest, a harmonium provided the musical accompaniment. Praise and prayer were robust when delivered by local preachers, who were known to all. The preacher must "keep to t'Good Book" or run the risk of being considered "modern" and challenged about his beliefs by senior members who awaited him in the vestry. A local preacher on trial was taken to task when he read his prayers, being told: "They should come from thi heart, not a scrap o' paper." As another young preacher was being led to the pulpit, the steward asked him if he was nervous. He nodded. "Nay, lad," whispered the steward, "we should be more nervous of thee than thou is of us."

Anglicans were less intense. One of them, an old chap, hearing an argument about religion, retorted: "If t'prayer book's reight – it's reight. If not, clap it at t'back o t'fire!" An old Keasden farmer who went to church "was a begger for going to sleep during t'service." The vicar included in his regular "announcements" details of anything that was missing. The old man woke up when he was announcing banns of marriage. Thinking that the vicar was referring to the farmer's two missing pigs, he said in a loud voice: "They're good to ken [recognise]. She's a black speck on her arse and he's new-gelded."

Hatches, Batches and Despatches – birth, marriage and death – were duly recorded in the church records. Courtship, between couples known to each other from schooldays, began when, after church or chapel or during a dance, a young man asked the lass if she would like to go for a walk. They were then considered to be "sweet on each other". If they linked hands, courting had begun. Unless a couple was "forced to wed", as someone would say, with a wink, courtship was protracted. When a dale-country farmer was told by a neighbour that "thy lad's got my lass into trouble", he replied: "He allus were clumsy. He broke a rake yesterday." One couple, who had been courting for a number of years, discussed their future. The lass said: "Isn't it time we got wed?" Said the not-so-young man: "Who'd hev us?"

For John Close, the family was "ready-made". He met and married Margaret, a widow with two daughters. Margaret turned out to be sour in her manner. As someone remarked: "He went round t'orchard and finished up plucking a crab apple." Willie Hargreaves, of Reeby's Farm, near Clapham, visited Polly King spasmodically. "She got fed up and wrote him a letter stating he'd either to "go right" or not at all. The way he was doing kept other men away. She "sharpened him up". He "went right" – and married her!

A farmer liked to think he was boss, but each family unit in this society was a matriarchy. He married a local lass, knowing she would have a will of steel, a practical outlook and no frills and fancies that would stretch the finances to breaking point. One chap fathered ten children – twice. He had two wives, yan at a time, of course. When one of the children died, another was conceived in the interest of numerical tidiness.

Getting married was "a bit of a palaver". Hence the delay to become legally bound. At the time of the Boer War, when a marriage was solemnised at Keasden, the bridegroom, a member of the numerous Wallbank family, was forty and his bride, Florrie Smith, was nobbut half that age. For the wedding, the farm women, who normally wore rough clothes and clattered about in clogs, appeared from their homes finely clad and, this being Victorian times, wore enormous hats that were inappropriate to an area of fierce winds and heavy rain. Gowns hung so low that when walking about they must be lifted up a little, saucily revealing more of their buttoned boots than was customary. The men were stiff and literally starchy in clothes that were infrequently worn and inclined to smell of moth-balls.

Florrie Smith was glad to be wed and on the great day the gamekeeper, Tom Pritchard, anticipating the passage of the bridal couple in their specially decorated horse and trap, stretched a broad ribbon across the road, from post to post. Written upon the ribbon were the words: "The Relief of Lady Smith." Florrie was not amused. For the journey to the reception at the *Flying Horse Shoe*, the main trap "had old shoes and bits of metal jingling behind." The newly-weds then crossed the road to the railway station and entrained for a honeymoon Morecambe, being seen off "with great gusto".

At least one wedding reception was held "on the baulks", the wooden flooring above the shippon in the big barn. The baulks were reached by climbing a cat-ladder. The celebration took place just before the cows were brought in for the winter; the place had been "swept and swept and swept" and the walls were "white-washed out" to ensure they were as clean as a new pin. The meal was "partaken of" by the light of paraffin lamps. The guests sat on bales of straw. The area was then cleared for dancing, to music played on a concertina. Grandma brought the supper in a huge basket. On offer were sandwiches, parkin and oatmeal cracknels plastered with home-made butter. Grannie had stood at the bottom of the cat-ladder and shouted for help. Willing hands grasped the basket, the huge cans of tea and the mugs into which it would be poured."

Nellie Swindlehurst, from Bracken Garth, was married at Clapham Church to Joseph William Parker of Longlands Farm. She was twenty-two years old; and he was thirty. It was the first day of June and there was a festive air. Charlie Coates, from the *Flying Horse Shoe*, drove the bridal pair from church to the hotel for the "wedding breakfast". Most of the others had to walk. "It came on rain – and it didn't half rain. We were soaked before we got to the *Shoe*."

At Coat Faw, in Cowgill parish, where Thomas James

Middleton and his wife reared a family of fourteen, the house was big enough for several wedding breakfasts. "One was me dad's uncle, another me dad's brother Joe, who was blind; he'd been kicked by a horse. Mrs Taylor, of Moss House, retained unhappy memories of her wedding day. She was nineteen years old and, as she said, "I was such a poor delicate lass they had to dress me for t'wedding." Yet she had a family of twelve and reared every one. It kept her busy. "I was that thrang I hadn't time to wesh mi hair."

A farm lad who managed to get a few days off for his honeymoon, and took his wife to Morecambe and Blackpool, was having the first real holiday of his life.

A big family was the norm because of a stern morality, the absence of reliable contraception and a high child mortality. One or two unofficial midwives were available. Old Nanny was as good a doctor as she was a vet. If a cow had difficulty when calving, the farmer would "fetch Old Nanny". And if t'doctor was unhandy, living miles away, Old Nanny would "tak ower" till he arrived.

In the pre-telephone age, it was known for a farmer to ride or jog-trot a few miles for the nearest doctor as his wife went into labour. The doctor employed a coachman, who would attend the horse and trap while he attended to the patient. If the doctor had to stay all night, the poor coachman had a restless time walking the horse about the yard to keep it and himself warm.

Good quality horses were maintained, but no horse could touch Maggie for speed. She was said to cover a mile in four minutes. The farmer who owned Maggie summoned the doctor and, on the return to the farm, overtook the doctor's nag. It was reckoned she had done a mile in three minutes. The first car that came into a rural area belonged either to the landowner or the doctor. In the case of the medical practitioner at Clapham, it was a big open Ford. When it was first driven to Keasden, children were allowed out of school to watch it pass. On the unmetalled road, it was trailing a cloud of lime dust.

Death looked over a child's right shoulder from the moment of birth. Thomas Victor, one of the Swindlehurst babies, died of pneumonia when he was six weeks old. At High Grain, on the moor-edge above Clapham, sixteen children were born and four died within a fortnight of each other from diphtheria. Their funeral cards were framed and displayed in the living room along with an embroidered homily: "God is Love". No one doubted that the children had gone to heaven.

## UNWILLINGLY TO SCHOOL

Some lads escaped the educational process. In Dentdale: "My dad only went to school for two days. They were takkin' in t'high fell. He had to go up there to keep t'sheep where they should be." The principal subjects were what became known as the Three R's – reading, (w)riting and (a)rithmatic. There were four R's if you added religion. Every schoolday began with prayers and the Vicar was a regular visitor. One day, while talking about the ladder, in Jacob's vision, he asked why the angels were using it. A lad from a dalehead farm said: "Appen they were in t'moult."

Children as young as five walked several miles, twice a day, to their lessons. The children from Cosh had a round trip of six miles to school at Halton Gill, where the teacher arranged for clothes to be dried off by the stove. She made toast for the farm children at dinnertime. Two of the girls from Cosh lodged at Halton Gill from Monday to Friday. One child, attaining the age of five, was kept at home until he was seven because no lodging place was available. The farm children living in Grisedale, a secluded valley at the head of Garsdale, crossed a moorland ridge – the boundary between West and North Ridings – to attend Lunds School. Kids from

Round Ing, the topmost farm, who set off at 8 a.m., had a two-mile walk. The Grisedale children met up with scholars from other farms until there was a chattering company of fifteen or so.

Schoolchildren had a uniform, of sorts. A schoolboy wore cap, shirt, jacket and fustian trousers with clogs on his feet. "We'd no fancy shoes." At dinner-time, a child from a remote farm might walk to the cobbler's shop to get some new clog-irons fitted. A girl's main attire was frock and pinafore. She also had clogs that were someone daintier than those made for a lad. A diversion on the way to school for the kids of upper Keasden was burning gorse bushes, just for fun. Gorse blazed spectacularly, "a real bonfire". If school lads put a match to a thicket of gorse during the mid-day break, the teachers were cross because the arsonists returned to their lessons with black hands that besmirched the school books. "If we burnt 'em on our way home, nobody said owt, for if gorse bushes became rank, sheep got tangled up in them."

The dale-country school of the Victorian type had an austere appearance, with windows set high to admit light without distracting the children by tempting them to look out of them. In some schools, heating was by coal fire at each end of a single room that might be divided into two if necessary. Otherwise there would be a centrally-placed stove. "It was so cold." Headmistresses were noted for their severity. "The cane was always there, ready to give you such a wallop if you got a sum wrong or if you dare to smile or talk to your neighbour. The cane used to come whistling down and make a big weal up your arm." A child broke the no-speaking-unless-spoken-to rule to tell the teacher, who habitually stood with her back to the fire, that her skirt was smouldering.

There were no catering facilities at school beyond a kettle. "We took sandwiches, pasty and cake. Unless we came across a bit of water in a gutter, we mun wait till we got home at night for a drink."

At one school, "some horrible tea was made with a kettle on a smoky fire." Kit Newhouse took a basin of porridge which became stiff and cold. The basin reposed in a handkerchief that had been knotted at four corners. His mother had given him "a bit o' sugar in some paper and a spoon." Kit would play with his porridge, flicking the basin from one hand to another. Another lad had a whole pasty that was wrapped in a handkerchief. He ate the pasty piecemeal, at playtime and dinnertime. If there was any pasty left when school closed, he swallowed it before setting off for home.

Fellside children had long holidays. "We stayed away from school when it was haytime. There was work for us to do. We were bored stiff raking up round the side of the meadow. My brother and me went 'turning' in what we thought was a big meadow. It would be only a few acres. Turn away, turn away, backwards and forwards, with my father saying: 'Look at that you've done, not at that you have to do'."

# HORSE POWER

When the horse was master of the dusty road, someone tried to sell a fine trap animal to Fred Cornthwaite of Rathmell, stating that it could cover a mile in four minutes. Fred replied: "Nay lad! Not with me!" He thought that was too fast.

Some farmers were especially good at "brekking in stags", young horses of about 15 hands. Known as "gallowa's", they were good at any heavy job. James Swindlehurst, of Bracken Garth, made t'place poor by his preoccupation with horse-breeding. "We never had a reliable work-horse because as soon as one got settled down, someone came along and bought it. We kept two mares so we could rear two foals every year. We'd sell a foal at two years old. A lot of them went to Appleby Fair. "My father was always breaking horses; he'd buy a stag [young unbroken horse] for about £12, break it in, keep it for about twelve months to get it to work, then sell it for £23 to £30. Money was scarce. He said you had to make a pound or two where you could."

From March to July, it was not uncommon to see a man leading a be-ribboned stallion along the road. This was the main mating season for horses. He was heading for a town like Settle or Bentham with an uncastrated stallion, known as an "entire". One of the men who toured the farms with a stallion – a fierce animal – had one arm amputated from the elbow. In place of his arm he had an iron contraption, terminating in a hook. He slotted the hook through the stallion's halter and walk with it for miles. If he lodged at a farm on his travels, he had to pay for his board and for the stallion's keep.

John Close, of Dovenanter, Keasden, kept a Shire and the type known as a "farmer's handy". The big horse got belly-ache [inflammation] and John, who loved the animal, was so upset he stopped travelling, having the other horse castrated. If the service of an entire was needed after July, the farmer took his mare to the place where the stallion was kept.

Few people saw a horse foal. It was the shortest birth process imaginable. A farmer would get up in a morning and find that a foal had already been born and was standing – albeit, a little shakily – on its stilt-like legs. "I once saw a horse scratchin' t'grund. It didn't scratch many minutes before it went down, thrusting for all it was worth. It was soon foaled. If there was any trouble about the foal suckling, we plastered the mare's teats wi' treacle. A foal soon got the taste of it – and sucked." A foal born about May would run with its mother until October.

Many foals were broken in at two years old but if they were going to be worked regularly it was advisable to leave them until they were three. The owner put on the breaking gear, which included a bit with tassles attached. The horse would be constantly chewing at these. When the horse was "mouthed". Side-reins and a girth were introduced and the animal was walked. Then the long reins came into use and they began to be driven. "A week or two after that, the horse would be yolked to a chain harrow or a piece of wood and allowed to trail it up and down. Some horses were very good and some were the devil possessed. One or two could not be relied on and even after a year or two you had to watch them or they would be self-willed."

A June fair for work-horses took place at Bentham. Buying a horse was chancy. "You might get one that would not pull an ounce. One chap was landed with a dozen horses and not one of them was able to pull an empty cart out of a yard. Folk had sold him all the wrong 'uns." If a horse had too much dry keep, it became "brokken-winded" and spent much of its time puffing and blowing. There was no certain cure. "If you were careful and fed it on softer stuff, it were a lot better. But you couldn't cure it."

A farm horse that spent much of the early summer on rough pastureland was given additional feed at the approach to haytime. Oats and bran put the sheen back on its coat and a sparkle into its eye. Then the farmer took it to the nearest smith. Before the Great War, horses taken to Taylors at Green Smithy had new shoes fitted for six shillings. Haytime was a smith's busiest season and queues developed of farmers with horses who had left the shoeing process to the last minute. A farmer called Tommy would leave Doris, his horse, at the smithy and go home to another Doris, his wife, who provided him with a cup of tea. The smith was amused. "When we had nearly finished shoeing the horse, it would start to whinny, which meant that Tommy was on his way back. We couldn't hear him coming but, sure enough, in next-to-no-time he'd be in sight."

Horse fairs were held in most districts. At Bentham, the June Fair was for work-horses presented just before haytime when a good horse was a necessity. Buying a horse was chancy.

A good horse had a working life spanning some twenty years. Others "got done soon on" and were taken to the knacker's yard.

*Above:* Harry Cockerill and his piano accordion.
*Below:* Hawes in Victorian times.

*Above:* Appraising the pig at a Keasden farm.

*Below:* Stable yard at Malham Tarn House.

*Above:* Hand-knitters at Dent and Settle.

*Below:* Goose-plucking at a hill farm near Clapham.

*Above:* The old stone bridge in Langstrothdale, 1900.

*Below:* Keasden on sheep-washing day.

*Above:* Sheep-clipping.

*Below:* Filling a back-can with water from the river Swale.

*Above:* Transporting milk at Muker, 1900.
*Below:* Haymaking with horse and sled in Wensleydale.

*Above:* Young haymaker, Walden.

*Below:* Rowing-up in a Wensleydale hayfield.

The transport revolution.
*Above:* A Walden farmer on his "lile grey Fergie."
*Below:* Collecting milk for the dairy at Hawes in Wensleydale.

# THE MIGHTY BLACKSMITH

You remembered most of all the glow from t'smiddy fire; then the wheezy sound of the leathern bellows being operated to fan the flames. The blacksmith, fitting a hot shoe to the hoof of a horse, stood momentarily in a cloud of acrid smoke. Someone told a Dales smith that smoke was good for asthma. He replied: "Anybody who can smell that stuff hasn't got asthma."

The blacksmith worked to a fine tolerance. Some of the big horses had three-quarters of an inch of space for driving in a nail." The type of shoe for Dales horses was heel-and-toe which offered more wear and a better grip than the average shoe. When he was asked to shoe a stag [unbroken horse] it was "blood for money."

The first time I called at t'awd smithy at Gunnerside, in Swaledale, was just before haytime in 1952. Willie Calvert told me that he and his son had shod fourteen horses in a single day. The farms were being mechanised but horses – mainly t'Dales Galloways – were still needed on steep ground. The building seemed packed with metal tools, some shiny with use and others tacked to the beams, where they were resting amid gossamer-like veils of cobwebs. Some, such as the docking-irons used to remove horses' tails, were recognisable as implements and others were strange contraptions that a versatile blacksmith had devised to meet particular needs.

The blacksmith performed some of the remedial work now undertaken by a vet. He had "flems", which were used in conjunction with a wooden mallet for tapping the veins when it was necessary to "bleed" a horse. He gathered fuzz-balls, a type of fungi, and used the dry spores to staunch the bleeding. If a farmer brought a horse suffering from inflammation of the hoof, such as might be caused by a nail, the old-time smith would rest the hoof on his knee and apply pressure all round, using a pair of pincers, until the horse "flinched". He knew where the puss had gathered. He "gouged in" with a knife until he saw a dark mark that he followed down to where the pressure could be released. The work done, the hoof was sealed using Stockholm tar that had been warmed and was allowed to run in."

Some horses were bow-legged or knock-kneed. Others had become pincer-toed. Hooves might show evidence of disease such as laminitis. A good blacksmith could correct the gait of an animal that was not "walking right."

On a winter day, as darkness came, a Dales blacksmith might set to work making a few shoes. He'd simply rough 'em out. Then he'd put them on pegs attached to the beams so that next summer he'd have some shoes ready for the haytime rush. The shoeing-house might hold two horses. At Settle, you could gamble on Dicky Taylor, of Armitstead Hall, sending two horses on a wet day when haytime work was temporarily halted. The smith often got soaked from working with a wet horse.

Will Hodgson, of Dent, would arrive at Settle with a consignment of scythes. He had long-poled scythes with blades five feet or so long for farmers who wanted to mow meadowland. The smaller Yankee scythe had a curved shaft. Jim Hodgson knew how to "lay in" a Kendal pole. You matched it to the man, taking into account his size and asking him to kick his leg out to assess his stride.

The farmers got value for money. At Settle, Alf Limmer's first job was removing the shoes. "When it came to hammering them on, I'd pick up a nail only to hear the farmer say: 'You're not going to prick it, are you, Alf? Are you getting enough 'od? It's going to stop on, is it?" With such comments, it is a wonder that Alf had any confidence left to drive a nail in. "But you got used to the chatter in time."

The apprentice blacksmith was taught how to drill a square hole through the roller of a mangle needed for wash-day. A dribble was used, which meant it could be drilled from each side. Having made an incense carrier for the Catholic priest, a blacksmith priced the job at £30. The priest gave him £33, stating that he would not give any charge connected with the figure thirty, "because Our Lord was betrayed for thirty pieces of silver."

Burn-marks on the woodwork beside the door indicated where the smith, having made stamps to be heated for marking sheep horns, had been "proofed" to check their accuracy. In the Gunnerside smithy, I saw a mould used for locally-produced lead. This was marked Old Gang and had the initials AD, which were possibly those of Ann Draycott, who had owned the mineral rights and claimed royalty on every pig of lead that left the district. David Calvert, grandfather of Willie, had done work for the Whitaside Mining Company. In the old days, coal for the forge came from the shallow pits on Tan Hill or Stockdale, being carted down to Gunnerside in five hundredweight loads. "It was not very good quality. What they wanted was good, clean coal because it was fire-welding and the coal had to be free of slag."

At Settle, the Hodgsons used coke from the gasworks. Billy Hartley from Swainstead delivered four or five bags of Monkton coke every fortnight, having collected them from Mr Hickling, the gasworks foreman. Now and again he'd buy Old Hickling a pint in the King Billy [William IV pub] and a hundredweight bag was more likely to weigh nearer two hundredweights. Monkton coke was special and "when you were welding wrought-iron, you could work for hours before you got a clinker." The blacksmith usually made the "carkers" for clogs. He shod both the men and the horses.

# BEST FOOT FORWARD

Many a farmer and some of the postmen clattered about in clogs, which were ideal for turning t'snaw broth [slush during the thaw]. Goose-grease was used to waterproof boots, which were usually worn by farmers at the action mart.

A cobbler's shop was a cal 'oil [gossiping place]. The fire in an iron stove was never allowed to go out and so his premises were small and cosy. Warmth had seeped into the walls. Within living memory, a pair of new shoes, made to measure and hand-stitched, cost one guinea. Good boots cost "rayther more".

Clog soles were from alder or birch. Tom King of Keasden bought standing trees, felled them, cut them into blocks and stacked them in such a way the drying breezes would pass between them. Men's clogs were of the type that laced up. Those for women were secured by clasps. Tom made coloured clogs – red or blue – for children.

The Kings, father and son, were full of mischief. One of their callers, Robby Wilshaw, habitually arrived late at night when, after a busy day, they were breaking off for supper. Robby usually outstayed his welcome. They hit on a plan to discourage him. Bob slipped into the house, collected a white tablecloth, darted a few yards along the road to the churchyard and waited for the visitor to begin his walk home.

As footsteps were heard, he put the tablecloth over his head and appeared above wall level. Robby, seeing "something spectral", did not bolt for home, as was intended, but took an easy operation. Turning on his heels, he returned to the home of the King family, which was adjacent to the shop. The cobbler had to accompany the terrified man to his farmhouse home.

PART THREE

# *High Summer*

*In retrospect, the peak of the year seemed little more than a blink between two long winters. It tended to be dull and moist. As the meadow grass grew lustily, in unaccustomed warmth, it provided cover for the immigrant corncrake, which came to vocal life after dark, keeping many people awake as it serenaded the moon with its monotonous double call, crex, crex. Flies swarmed at the muck-middens. Horse-flies, known as clegs, sent the cows into a frenzy of movement known to the dalesfolk as "gadding".*

*At haytime, as the young men worked "every hour God sends", old men donned their keitels [cotton jackets] and Panama hats and recalled arduous days making hay in fitful summer sunshine. They had risen at 3 a.m. and were ready to mow at first light. Horses pulled the mowing machines and must not be worked during the heat of the day. Haytime meals include sandwiches, cake and big pasties.*

*In a fine spell, a whirlwind might send wisps of hay spiralling upwards. This was a portent of rain within three days. When it rained incessantly at the wrong time, a farmer tapped his barometer with the gusto of a woodpecker rapping a dead tree. Owd Ben was taken ill; there was no thermometer in the house, so the barometer was laid on his chest. When t'needle spun to "dry", they gave him a sup o' watter.*

*Cotton grass whitened the upland bogs as though with summer snow. In due course, the normally dour moorland wore its Joseph's coat of many colours. Bell heather, in clumps, was attired in regal purple. With the flowering of the link, it was as though a purple carpet had been laid – a fitted carpet: all the way to the horizon.*

# BUTTER AND CHEESE

Dales farmers kept the Shorthorn breed of cow, a dual purpose animal, yielding good quality milk and fine beef. The Shorthorn might be white or red or a mixture known as "roan" which was much favoured. A Shorthorn was generally healthy but if "owt ailed it" medicine was administered as a two-man job, one holding a cow horn into which the medicine had been poured and the other keeping the animal's mouth open. If a cow was "coughing and spluttering", a red drench was administered.

Each cow was fed separately, using provin from its own wooden bucket. The traditional mixture consisted of a shovelful of "thirds", a shovelful of bran and a shovelful of Indian meal, to which was added water drawn from the well in a zinc bucket, the whole being stirred by a wooden stick known as a thible. Each bucket was lifted from the foddergang into the boose, where a cow was standing, lightly tethered from the neck.

Milking was by hand. It was a knack developed by a lad as his schooldays came to a close. If a young lad was milking, another would say: "Gie us a squirt." The milker would send a jet of milk towards him. The skill lay in working the hands. It was said that cows liked to be milked by a lady because she exerted a firm but gentle grip udder. A cow was prone to kick a man or at least to swish its tail so that muckbuttons [hardened pieces of dung] lacerated his face. Milk that squirted noisily against the side of a two-gallon bucket eventually overflowed the bucket as froth that carried with it bits of muck. Milk intended for sale was poured into a sile tin, thence through various sieves to ensure there were no foreign bodies. Not that anyone bothered. A Dentdale farmer was heard to say: "Milk tastes o' nowt until t'cow's had its foot in t'bucket."

A farm dairy stood on the north side of the house, which rarely had direct sunlight. In the dairy were binks [broad shelves], many of them formed of Helwith Bridge blue-flag. The floor was covered by close-fitting pieces of flagstone. This little room was so cold that eggs froze in winter.

Blue-flag was ideal for a foodstuffs, being impervious to liquid and easily cleaned. On the main ledge were placed the galvanised trays called leads. Into them was poured milk fresh from the cow. When the cream naturally separated, adhering to the sloping sides, a plug was withdrawn and the "blue" milk drained off, to be fed to the calves.

The cream, scraped from the sides of the "lead", was placed in a crock to await butter-making. In the dairy of a farm at Wharfe, near Austwick, "we had three binks that were regularly washed." A farmer's wife who was particular [house-proud] mixed some blue milk with water to give them a gloss. More than one farmer's wife used dishes for the milk; when the cream had separated she rested the edge of the dish on the cream pot and, with a finger, skimmed off the cream.

The best sort of butter was made at fog-time, when cattle were ingesting the second crop of grass, the first having been converted into hay. The farmer brought in a bucket of milk and his wife sieved it before pouring it into the leads. In winter, you let the milk stand "three meals" whereas in summer, when there was a risk of it souring, it "stood two". You did not get as much cream off, but t'calves got the benefit.

The old folk remember using the end-over-end churn, which could be hard work, especially to any child who was asked to turn the handle. If it was coldish weather, you put the cream near the fire to ripen. If the cream was at a good average temperature, you might churn for about twenty minutes; otherwise it could take an hour and a-half. To ease the task and create the right speed, a hymn might be sung, a favourite being *Onward Christian Soldiers*. In summer, the churner might be operating for two hours before a slapping sound on the side of the churn or a jerking of the handle indicated that curdling had taken place. "When you got tired of churning, you peeped at the little glass window at one side to see if it was clearing. When it cleared, it was butter."

Desperate measures were sometimes demanded. The churner might add a pint of boiling water or a handful of salt to the mixture. If a lad who was churning was inattentive, he might get the handle under his chop [chin].

With the churning ended, the operator then took off the handle, drained off the butter-milk and brought out the butter, a big golden slab, into a butter-bowl that had been scalded then chilled with cold water. It was now time to use Scotch Hands [wooden bats with short handles]. A handful of butter was placed on a slab of slate and patted into shape, putting some "fancy jitters" across the top as a decorative effect. When round pounds of butter were required, a circular wooden print, of sycamore, which did not taint the butter, was stamped on top as a mark of the place of origin. "Grannie, who could do anything with butter, such as plaiting it, kept some back at harvest festival time. She made a fancy basket, containing eggs with a hen sitting on them – all in butter. It looked lovely when it was set up in church on a white doyley." An old woman attending a butter-making class could "mak nowt" of Scotch Hands and reverted to using her hands. Butter was taken to market, much of it being en route for dealers in industrialised towns, in butter-boxes, each holding thirty or forty-five pounds. In hot weather, it was kept cool by being wrapped in rhubarb leaves. The quality of an individual's butter depended largely on the type of ground on which the cattle were grazed. Some farms were noted for fine butter. Others, from inferior areas, might not be able to sell all their butter. On market day, a luckless woman would be seen standing in a pitiful rank, shame-faced and fretful because no one wanted her butter.

Wensleydale and adjacent valleys were famed for their farmhouse cheese. The milk was raised to a specific temperature and rennet was added. It was stirred for about a quarter of an hour, when it began to curdle. "It went into a beautiful sort of jelly. I left it for a quarter of an hour, when I got a large carving knife and cut the jelly into squares, first one way, then another." The curds and the whey were formed. The whey was drained off and the curds were crumbled up, adding some salt, then pressing it into vats, which resembled "huge cake tins with holes in", leaving it under pressure until it was dry and firm before stitching it round with white cotton.

## RUSH GATHERING

Bracken and rushes were cut and carted as bedding for young stock in winter. You could mow bracken when it was greenish and leave it strewn about the fellside for a week or two until it turned into a bronze hue. In a dry season, a farmer ran the risk of leading his horse and mowing machine on to mossland, where it was level and tufts of rushes were dense. "T'grund fair shacked [shook]" and you hoped you didn't break through t'crust and get bogged.

Above Bare Bell, at the head of Keasden, was a powerful spring called Bullock's Well. It surged from a benty [grassy] hillside. The men who passed it when they were sleddin' bedding [bracken] on hot autumn days looked forward to drinking from it. "It was that cold it fairly cut t'back o' thi throat," said one of them. Normally, a scythe was employed to cut rush-bobs. The rushes were then forked loose on to a horse-drawn cart or sled to be stacked under cover. "If a tramp asked to stay in t'barn for t'neet, we'd give him a sup o' tea and some bread and jam. He preferred to lie on bracken rather than rushes; it was warmer."

When rush-gathering, a farmer did not have a specific area in mind. "If you got there early, you mowed a patch."

Rushes were "bad to cut and bad to get off. We sometimes had to carry armfuls of slippery rushes a long way to where we could get a horse and sled. Three or four of us were loading rushes, not far apart, when a horse got into a bog. It was right fast. Old Close, who never let anything worry him, went to it and said: 'You old begger; you've got yourself fast and you'll have to wait till I'm ready to get you out.' Nowt alarmed him. He sat down, got his bacca out and puffed away. Horse was fast up to t'belly. We had to get some bedding under it and roll it over to get it out."

Old Willie mowed "little bits, a few bats here and a few bats there. Then he ran somewhere else and mowed a few more." His greedy idea was to claim all the beds of rushes. His neighbours decided to frustrate him. When he was not present, they mowed all the remaining beds of rushes and took them away. "Old Willie arrived with a horse and sled at a time when the other farmers were about to start a grouse drive, a time usually avoided by farmers in deference to the sportsmen. "T'owd chap had fastened his 'oss to t'sled with a rope round its neck. As he came over t'hill, we all started waving and shouting. His horse struck off, galloping down t'fell, trailing t'sled bi t'neck. Willie, who had a squeaky voice, shouted: 'I won't come again. I won't come again'."

A horse-drawn sled was a necessity on the sloping land of the dalehead, where most of the lile farms were to be found. A great sled-maker in the Three Peaks area was Bob 'Ooson [Robert Howson, of Clapham]. Some people marvelled at his work but he was a true craftsman. He did not claim to be one, observing: "A sled's nobbut a gate on its side." When a laden sled was ready to be moved, a man held the horse while the other was hooking traces. "I'd got one trace on when something frightened t'hoss and it jumped sideways, so a trace was fast under its belly. It started kicking. Then it went round and round, kicking all the while, till there wasn't one rush left on t'sled. When we'd calmed t'hoss down, we had to load t'sled again."

# AT THE PEAT-POTS

The winter fuel on fellside farms was peat, not coal, unless you lived near where a coal seam outcropped as part of the Yoredale Series of rocks, high on the fells, and you could buy a cartload cheaply. Coal was reserved for special occasions. A farmer who bought five hundredweights when he moved to a dalehead holding had most of it left when he "flitted" a dozen years later.

Peat warmed you twice – when cut and stacked it on the moor and when you sat up to it on a winter night. The right to cut peat, known as turbary, was zealously guarded. "We had it on our deeds – we could take rushes for bedding and peat for burning." A peat-pit was opened up in May when the top layer of sods and soil was stripped off neatly, to be replaced when a season's pearting was over. This avoided wind-erosion. Gathering peat was in part a social event. "Ivverybody went to t'peat-grund. Come dinnertime and you all sat together and talked about this and that. Then you'd get up and do a bit more."

It was a repetitive, dusty job. "It took a lot of peat to keep the home fires burning 'cos peat is fast-burning stuff. We used to set off to t'moor at eight o' clock. We took drinking [a morning snack] and a bit of three o'clock. We'd stop on the moor till about half past six and then walk back. We hadn't a watch so we stuck a stick in the ground, then another stick a little way off. When the shadow of the first reached the second, it was time to go home." A lad who had got "fed up" with the work moved one of t'sticks a lile bit, which mean that the family arrived back home half an hour early.

If the peat-face was deep, a dyke was made to lower the water table. Like the human body, a turve of peat was mainly water, being sodden, almost like paste. The flat-bladed turf-spade, known as a slane, had a turned-up section along one edge. Cutting was undertaken vertically, the turve averaging six by nine inches with a thickness of four inches. The diggers sometimes came across the preserved remains of trees. An ancient forest had been smothered during a subsequent wet period when material that did not rot in the normal way formed the peat layer.

A farmer aimed to have all his peats cut and laid out, to harden and oxydise in the moorland breezes, by the 20th of June. A turf-barrow, made of ash by the local joiner, had a single broad wheel that did not readily sink in soft ground. It was said of a feckless joiner: "His peeart-barrows run as well as his water-butts."

After a week or two, peats were set on edge, one leaning against another, and the drying process continued. Many peats were formed into stacks shaped like old-fashioned bee-skeps, with gaps to admit the drying breezes. Then, with haytime over, it was time to transport the peat to the farmstead. "We usually managed to move four loads in a day." If a farm did not have a peat-house, a stack was made, then covered by large stones or slabs or peat, set at an angle so that rain would run off. In a good year, a man might build stacks with peat that was drying faster than he could cart it."

# OFF WITH THE WOOL

About a fortnight before sheep were clipped, they were washed to remove dirt and the last traces of the salve applied to their skins in November. A farmer might get two or three pence more for his wool if it had been washed. On the other hand, washed wool was lighter – and payment was on weight. At washing time, they "demmed t'beck" with an old door, with sacks and sods, at what was known as a wash-dub. Sheep were retained in a walled enclosure.

The sheep were delivered to the washer by the simple process of tossing them, one at a time, into the water. A sheep must be "head first and hinder-end uppards. Then went t'head came up, you got your arm under it and put the other hand on to t'rump and tipped it ower." The washer was standing chest deep in chilly beck water. "I've washed for up to five hours at a time. I didn't mind it as long as I had something to do, but if you scrambled out as you waited for the next lot o' sheep, then went back in again – it did cap you!"

The water should be "well up" the washer for if the level was low "t'back feet o' t'sheep would catch t'ground and that'd send you back'rds rooad in t'watter. If it was a mucky sheep, you'd hear the chap say: 'Give it a good do – it's a mucky-arsed 'un.' You'd give that a right good do, till you could see t'green rising up in t'watter. You washed the belly, then turned it to wash both sides." The sheep was then allowed to scramble out on the far bank, to dry off in the summer sunshine.

The washer was entitled to a nip o' whisky – unless he was of Methodist persuasion. A fanciful tale told at Keasden related to the day when the dogs were missing. The men set off for the dub, only to find their dogs had already rounded up the sheep. Moreover, one dog was throwing sheep into the water where another dog was washing them. Someone asked what the tale-teller's dog was doing. He replied: "It's going round wi' t'whisky."

At the dub in Crummockdale, above the hamlet of Wharfe, near Austwick, the men who did the washing were naked. Women arriving with food and drink prudishly left them behind a wall. Normally, women from the various farms brought baskets of food to a handy place at the side of the wash-dub. "They used to vie with each other as to who could take most. There were always some ham sandwiches and also gooseberry pies. At washing time, berries were ready."

If one chap had not quite finished washing his sheep, others would help out so that all went for the meal at the same time. As greasy water from the washing ran down the beck, "you'd see fish coming up to get air. Some of t'lads, when they'd had their dinner, took their dinner-tins down t'beck and filled 'em wi' trout."

At the big farms, they had a "boon clip", so called because farmers of adjacent holdings collaborated and clipped the flocks in turn. There was no bigger "boon" than at Catlow, which spread itself some 800 ft above sea level at the wild head of the Hodder Valley. At the edge of living memory, twenty or thirty clippers were kept busy. They sat on benches known as "stocks" and took their sheep from helpers who were known as "catchers". They did the running about, also re-marking the animals and rolling up the fleece in a traditional way that used part of it as the binding. The custom faded away as recently as the 1950s when it was getting harder to attract clippers. "We didn't like to clip much before July and they wanted to make hay then."

Everyone enjoyed the Wallbank Clip at Keasden Head. "When we'd clipped a good while, Will Wallbank would say: 'You've done terrible weal, chaps. Let's a' summat to eat.' Then we kept on clipping till we'd done... You got well-fed. And that's all you got! No one thowt of asking for pay. They kept coming round with sandwiches, pasties and tea or beer." T'owd men drank home-distilled gin. Hired men drank home-made beer.

The clip took in a number of family farms and several thousand sheep, including a host of old wethers [sheep castrated as lambs and kept several years for the wool]. "I've known when there were twenty-six of us clipping. Most of them used stocks [special benches] but some clipped on t'grund." A man who was a poor clipper, forever nicking the sheep with his shears, would be switched to wrapping wool.

There wasn't a mad-rush to clip. Those who smoked pipes broke off now and again to do just that. Others reflectively chewed black twist. They'd clip a sheep or two. Then have a talk. Somebody counted all the folk up at the dance that followed the clipping. There were ninety-three. Sheep that could not be clipped because the new wool had not risen were turned off and another attempt to clip them made a week later.

At about ten o' clock, when the last sheep was clipped, a big meal was served. "A great lump o' beef was produced and supported by plenty of vegetables. Then there'd be puddings and pies. After that, we danced on t'flag floor till one or two o' clock in t'morning. We danced to Johnny Harrison, who had a concertina. He'd stand in a corner and pull such awful faces. There was just him and Bob Wallbank with a fiddle. We thought that was plenty. Then you'd to walk home, getting there about three o' clock. T'wommin didn't care much for us when we'd been among t'sheep all t'day and sweating. We stunk!"

A cold snap could be bad for the sheep. Norman Swindlehurst related: "I've only known one lot of sheep starve [chill] to death in my life. It was at High Birks, when a chap called Johnson was there. He'd got them in the night before so they'd be dry. We hadn't to clip 'em damp, otherwise they [the woolmen] knocked so much a pound off. We clipped all day till late at night. They'd nothing in their bellies. It came on a terribly wild, wet day. He took 'em through t'gate on to t'moor and next morning there were twenty-one lying dead against gate. They'd been that starved; they'd never been able to get to pasture. They'd just stood there till they dropped."

## HAYTIME

In July, the sweet, almost sickly smell of new-mown hay filled the air. One of the most aromatic of grass species was that known as Yorkshire fog. Summer mornings in a pastoral area like the Dales were a delight. Red grouse might be heard talking to each other on the nearby moor. The air resounded with the bubbling calls of curlews. The 14 acres of meadowland at Cosh were "a bit rough" and so were mown by scythe. A field gate was taken from its hinges and, horse-drawn, became a hay-sweep. The hay was transported to the barn by horse-drawn sled.

Each farmer was his own weather-forecaster. In chancy weather, he fretted. When the sun shone like a blow-torch he might he heard whistling, yet if the sun gleamed – too much, to early – it was glisky [unreliable]. In thundery conditions, haytime was a game of chance. At Malham, where a narrow valley separated two farms, a helper laid a bet with his fellow haymakers as to which would finish first. "We'd about four load each to get. Then we saw t'other lot running out of t'hayfield. Heavy rain! We never got a drop, so we finished first. That was thunder-weather for you." If the fells seemed close, it was bahn to rain. If cattle grazed high up, with light showing between their bodies and the ground, it'd be aw reight.

A Dentdale lass, aged nine, "could do owt in a hayfield – load a sledge or a cart or owt. When I was supposed to be at school, I was leading hay wi' t'horses." Haytime for the women began a week or two before the first mowing. The pantry was stocked for the expected large labour force who'd want summat to eat every few hours through the working day. Two barrels of beer formed a special requirement for the men, and especially for the Irish helpers. If beer was home-made, it must not be "dish-washy stuff". Ginger beer in stone bottles assuaged the thirst. Nettle beer, being cheap, was made in large quantities. Mason's Extract was a herbal preparation that must be "let down" before being bottled. It was powerful stuff and every year corks left some of the bottles with the velocity of bullets – or the bottle burst. Elderflower "champagne" was said to be good for the blood. One of the Wallbank family of Keasden distilled whisky.

A Craven farmer's wife remembered when her mother made a huge bowl of lemon-water – "two gallons at a time." Half a dozen fresh lemons were cut up and placed in the bowl with a goodly quantity of sugar, a spoonful of cream of tartar and perhaps a few sticks of rhubarb, these last two giving it a tang. Boiling water was poured over the mixture, the pieces of lemon floated temptingly and anyone who wished to drink used a cup that stood beside the bowl. A townie married to a fellside farmer, hearing that lemon water was a refreshing haytime milk, bought pounds of lemons and used a seventeen gallon milk kit. "Then the weather broke down and it was all wasted."

The farmer usually hired one or more of the Irishmen from County Mayo, in the west of Ireland, who for many years, and especially before the Great War, helped out on the dale-country farms. The custom of Irish labour continued on a smaller scale after the war. They were sometimes called "July Barbers" and each was hired at a figure that included food, lodgings and – essentially – a barrel of ale. They were rarely well paid and never over-paid, receiving £8 or £10 for the contracted month. It was agreed that if haytime finished they could leave before the month end. Michael Brett and

John Prendergast turned up at a Craven farm year after year. Then Michael began to bring his two sons. They slept on straw beds in a spare room that held a chest of drawers, a chair and a few pegged rugs on the floor.

The mowing was done with the aid of a scythe of awesome appearance and potential. It was straight-shafted, with a blade almost as long as a man was tall. Four men, working as a team, mowed an acre in the best part of two hours. A Keasden man born in 1902 remembered a haytime when there were two gangs of eight scythesmen – sixteen men, some regular, some Irish who were over for t'summer. "They moved yan behint t'other, 'im that could mow t'quickest going last. Those who didn't get a move on in front had their heels cut into. It med 'em go. There were no slackin'. Both gangs met up in t'last field, which was about three acre. They had to concentrate and work as a team, 'cos ivverybody mewed [mowed] different." *Wheeeew!* You could hear the blade passing through the grass. A good scythesman reckoned to mow a yard in at a time.

Attached to the shaft of the long-shafted scythe was a strickle, a four-sided length of wood pitted with many holes. The strickle gave the scythe balance. Without it, it would be "head heavy" and the lay [blade] would go down into t'ground. Smeared with bacon fat, the strickle was dusted with fine sand to provide an abrasive surface for putting a fresh edge on the blade. A farmer might buy some scythe sand, which was fine and hard, or get his own from the shore of a felltop tarn. Another source was burning pieces of sandstone in the fire until they were reddy-orange, when they were "brayed i'bits". Jim Metcalfe, working for Jack Coates at Low Trenhouse, on Malham Moor, was asked to climb Fountains Fell with a biscuit tin and bring back a load of fine white sand from beside the tarn. The tin was so heavy that on his return to the farm he kept putting it down so that he could rest. John Akrigg's first scythe was taller than he was and he had to look up when sharpening the blade. The sand used for dusting the strickle came from the side of one of the Whernside tarns. "I'd set off for sand one night after I'd milked. Me and my brother once got more than we bargained for, so we tipped some sand out afore we got far."

One man's scythe may have been assembled in the previous season. The farmer had provided the various parts. After haytime, it was hung up in the barn to await the labourer's return. The Old English scythe was supplanted by the American variety, known as a Yankee, which was smaller and had a curved shaft. A conservative farmer might remark: "Oh, he's getten a Yankee scythe – he'll mow damn all wi' that."

The Irishmen tended to be heavily dressed, with heavy woollen vest and long-legged underpants, covered by durable clothing. At one farm, the heat proved too much for one man, who died. "He just dropped down dead in the hayfield. Not another bat of work did his friends at this and some other farms do for a while. They took him to one of the outbarns, demanded a barrel of beer and sat round him, day and night, burning candles." The farmers ran through a gamut of emotion at the hold-up – and the prevailing hot weather.

On wet days, when no haytime work was possible, an Irishman was set to work doing menial jobs, such as mowing thistles, cleaning out calf boxes, weeding cobbles or white-washing the interiors of outbuildings, a process known as "bug-blinding". Other specialist tasks were replacing defective teeth on wooden rakes or stuffing fleeces into wool-bags for despatch to Bradford, thus clearing space for the year's crop of hay.

An Irishman arrived at a farm with a few possessions in an attache case and carrier bag. He emerged from his quarters on a Sunday morning wearing his best clothes – white shirt, blue suit, brown shoes or boots. He then walked to the nearest Catholic church to attend Mass. Afterwards, he might resort with his friends to a hostelry. When he returned to the farm, he and his pals were a little unsteady on their feet.

When Norman Swindlehurst was eighteen years old, he hired at Chapel House, Newby, and was paid thirty shillings for a month's work. He went the year afterwards and got fifty shillings. They had two meadows on the roadside going towards Clapham. "We always did hand-milking and took milk to Clapham station to catch the half past seven train. My boss said we must be up early in the morning. He wanted to mow the little meadow before we went to milk. We had an oil lantern fixed on the machine. We just got into t'field and Clapham church clock struck one. We worked till ten at night."

An early start was made so the horse would not have to work during the heat of the day. Mary Boothman related: "The hay days were always so hot. Even when it was morning, the horses would be steaming – so soon in the day. It was my job to take Grandad's breakfast to him in the meadow. It had to be there at eight o' clock. There'd be a steaming bowl of porridge and on top of that a plate of bacon and eggs. I also took a can of tea." On such mornings, one might almost be overwhelmed by the smell of new-mown grass and by the bubbling calls of curlews.

Haytime was hard on men and horses. Inexperienced men who were "helping out" developed water-blisters on their hands. The young horses were apt to become sore about the shoulders through profuse sweating. The remedy was to bathe those shoulders with salt and water. Or to fill old stockings with hay and use them as pads, protecting the horse against rubbing by the harness.

Extra corn was purchased for the horse at haytime. It must not, for its health's sake, be allowed to dine on new hay. In the evening, midges formed tawny clouds. Or someone would find what appeared to be a small black grape adhering to one of his legs. A sheep-tick, bloated with blood, should not be flicked off or its head would remain buried under the skin and a septic leg could result.

When the first horse-drawn mowing machines appeared, it was usually the Irishman, with his long-shafted scythe, who "broke out" the edges of a field, allowing unimpeded access for the mechanical mower. The old-time crops were relatively light, the grass being near to seeding, and so the simple type of mowing machine was not overwhelmed. Grass was most easily cut when the dew was upon it, another reason why a farmer should mow at first light. The wise farmer did not mow more in a day than he and his men were capable of loading in the same period of time. Given good weather, clearing a field was classically a three-day operation: the grass was cut one day, turned the next and gathered as hay on the third.

After the hay had been strawed [strewn] and then rowed-up, it was transferred to the barn. On fellside farms, this was achieved using horse and sled. An eleven-year-old schoolboy who got a holiday job as "sled lad" at Nether Lodge, near the head of Ribblesdale, was in charge of a Shire horse and the big wooden sled. Riding the horse along the rows, he stopped periodically as hay was forked on to it in a traditional way, using so many "rounds". He would then ride it to the barn. The laden sled was left and the horse was harnessed to an empty one. He slept in a big bedroom – big enough to accommodate three beds. A "jerry" stood in the middle of the floor. A Cumbrian augmented the labour force for haytime. He was good at catching rabbits and showed the young lad how to set snares, also how, with long pole to which a snare wire was attached, he could slip the noose over the head of a trout swimming idly in one of the pools at the river.

When a load of hay was to be transported from field to barn, stout ropes attached to the back of a cart were tossed over the load. Each in turn was pulled tight. The man who directed this operation stood on the cart and his voice rang out clearly: "Pull, pull, pull, pull – and tie!" At the barn, the hay was shifted by rake through the forking hole to what was variously known as the floor-mew or mewstead, where one or two men were ready to trample it down. Hay that was a bit "short of ready" finished up on "the baulks", above the byre. The best quality hay that was intended for the floor-mow might be on a horse-drawn cart that was backed into the barn for off-loading. Where there was a porch, the load came within inches of the timbers on which swallows would be nesting.

The wise farmer, when building up the mew, left small spaces through which it could sweat. In a week or so, steam would be seen rising from them. Hay that had been taken in "a bit short of dry" might fire. One couple went to the local show about three weeks after the completion of haytime. That was the crucial time for a barn fire. The farmer's wife recalled of her husband: "He kept looking back towards the farm to see if there was any smoke rising. He was a bit timid about the barn. The hay had gone in a bit quick!" Hay that was "almost ready to burn" was found to be black as it was cut out and dragged into the farmyard to avoid a fire.

The haytime meal (drinkings) consisted of a few sandwiches. One of the women went out with the food in an oblong woven basket and the tea in a can. During the day there'd be a meal with stew, made of beef or lamb. Many of the dalesfolk killed lambs for the kitchen. In the evening there would be a big hot meal. A lad who, during a hot afternoon, was sent back to the farm for a cold drink for the men was handed a heavy stone bottle containing home-brewed beer. "It was a fair weight for a lad of ten. And he'd a mile and a-half to walk. He was dry, so he took cork out. Then he had a drink. And, later, a few more drinks. Till he was drunk. He flopped on a grassy bank. The bottle rolled into the dyke. He couldn't get up – but he could hear t'beer glug, glug, glug, glugging out o' t'bottle. They sent some of t'Irishmen to look for him. The lad was hard and fast asleep.

Them Irishmen were a bit twined [annoyed]."

The old-time farmers were fussy about leaving a field clean; they did not want to see even so much as a wisp of hay on the land. Raking t'dyke bottoms was a common practice. If anyone found a tuft of bright green grass, a farmer who was not too fussy would say: "Purrit in wi' t'hay. It'll help it to sweat." Hay taken when it was rather damp, as it might be during a poor summer, soon gave the barn the humidity of a Turkish bath. In one longhouse type of farmhouse, where the barn was adjacent to the living accommodation, the hay in the barn might sweat so vigorously the wallpaper in the parlour became damp and began to peel off.

HOYLE '90

# SICKNESS AND HEALTH

No one summoned a doctor unless the situation was desperate. He had a nasty habit of charging for his services. Grandad, who had bronchitis "every winter that ever came", had his condition alleviated by a poultice, made from oblongs cut from an old blanket, with a filling of meal, bran or bread crumbs, applied to his chest as hot as could be borne. Grandma, who administered the poultice, was indifferent to her husband's wailing. Poulticing was hard work. Whoever took the hot one upstairs met another coming down with the old one. When a three-month-old baby had pneumonia, poulticing saved her life.

Often there was not enough time to summon a doctor and a local lady, self-taught in the skills of nursing, was brought in. The son of them one them recalled: "I heard a knock on t'door and a neighbour shouted: 'Missus, will you come? There's a baby at our house.' Off she'd go. If there was a death, they also called on mother to lay the dead person out properly." When folk were poorly, they might take some hot whisky and go to bed. A farmer's wife was unwell one Christmas Day. One of her family went hot-foot to see the doctor. His home was a couple of miles away. Medicine was mixed and brought back to the farm.

Tom Pritchard, the gamekeeper, an eccentric sort of a fellow, wasn't well. They sent for t'doctor, who made up a bottle of medicine. Someone went back to the doctor the next day and said Pritchard was worse. The doctor went to see him and asked to see the medicine. Pritchard said he'd taken it in one dose, adding: "I thowt if there was owt good in it, I'd let it be doing." It varra near killed him for there was a lot of poison in it.

Whooping cough might be alleviated by taking a child to the nearest lime kilns or standing a child in fumes from where men were laying tarmac on a road. There'd always to be a jar of goose grease handy. It would be rubbed on the chests of those who suffered from bad colds.

## AILING STOCK

Uncle Tom was poorly. He reached for some cattle medicine kept on a top shelf in a cupboard. His brother asked: "What's tha tekkin'?" He said: "I'se no idea but it'll cure summat." T'owd folk couldn't afford vets. Then, having summoned one, they had their own ideas about "what's wrang". An appreciative farmer specially rewarded the vet with "a slice or two o' bacon" or a dozen eggs.

The dry in-calf cows were kept in outbarns over the winter and nearby would be calves, the future recruits to the milking herd. A cow with a cough signifying tuberculosis had plenty of time, in perfect conditions, to infect the rest of the stock. Infected milk led to many childhood deaths.

An ailing horse was prescribed colic drench – half a dozen pints for the largest horses – along with two powders.

Parasitic bronchitis, commonly known as "husk", was a worrying complaint in the age before antibiotics. An afflicted calf, which had picked up a lungworm from its pasture, would be "nobbut middlin" or even "going back'ards". It repeatedly coughed. An early remedy in the era of the vet was to inject a smelly mixture containing turpentine and chloroform. In the subsequent violent coughing, the animal would eject the parasite.

# GROUSE-SHOOTING

Matt Cherry, who was born and reared in Upper Swaledale, lived so near the moors that in a severe winter he was not surprised to see a row of moorcock [red grouse] perched on the capstones of the garden wall. As a youngster, in a family of gamekeepers, Matt was sent to the moor to bray [beat] the snow with a besom and expose the heather on which the birds fed. Otherwise, it was said, the grouse would migrate down-country. Matt was taught how to "call" grouse. In November, when old birds paired, he would sit in a hollow behind a wall, at first light, imitating the call of a hen grouse to attract a swaggering cock bird. Grandfather "called" grouse using a smoker's pipe.

This bird, known to the dalesfolk as "moorcock" and commemorated in the name of several moor-edge inns, is suited to the peat-and-heather environment from which it rarely strays. A thick plumage insulates it from the cold and wet. The cock bird's plumage of rufous-brown is inconspicuous. Not so the bright red eye wattles that are inflated during courtship and when territory is in dispute. A female in good condition has a rich honey tone, which blends with its surroundings as it covers its nest like a feathered tea-cosy. In winter, grouse have coarse white feathering on their legs – something like avian "spats".

A grouse has a small head and a short bill, with which it plucks heather – food that passes through a gut specially adapted for dealing with tough, fibrous plant food. In July, red grouse also dine on the seeds of bent, a coarse species of grass, and on moorland fruits such as crowberry and bilberry. By autumn, few creatures stirred on the high ground beyond the moorland trinity: grouse, sheep and crows. In Victorian times, moorland that was part of the big estates, and dedicated to the well-being of grouse, was shot over with such gusto that what had been a sport had become mass slaughter. As men discharged loaded guns handed to them by their attendants, the barrels became almost too hot to handle. One man vied with another over the size of the day's bag of the resilient moorcock.

Grouse-shooting had undoubtedly been sport at the start of the century when landowners and their friends shot grouse "over dogs" that ranged ahead of the shooters and "pointed" to where the birds were lying. At Muker, on the extensive estate of Lord Derby, a shooting party consisted of one or two guns, a couple of gamekeepers and from six to eight dogs. They trudged over the heathery commons of Angram, Thwaite and Oxnop, and over Black Moor and Muker Edge, following the dogs that "pointed" recumbent grouse. The shooting party reported their modest bags as "moor game", which took in grouse, the occasional golden plover and snipe and an assortment of small mammals. Lord Stanley, who became the 13th Earl of Derby (and one of the founders of the London Zoo) was usually partnered by a Mr Legh, though the two men shot separately and, at the end of the day, compared results.

By the start of the twentieth century, and leading up to the Great War, which shattered the social structure of many big estates, driving was in vogue. A line of beaters startled the grouse and sent them headlong to the area where shooters were concealed in butts until the last moment, when they filled the air with shot.

Gamekeepers were in charge. They were devoted to destroying "vermin" – foxes, stoats, crows and any bird with a hooked beak. A mini-army of farm men advanced in crescent-shaped formation, shouting and waving flags, causing the grouse to form large packs and driving them to the butts, where they must flew through a hail of cartridge pellets. After a day's shoot, cart loads of birds were transported from the moors to the big house and the surplus were taken by game dealer to market.

Before a shooting lodge was built at Keld, near the head of Swaledale, parties of grouse-shooters stayed in Kirkby Stephen and were conveyed to the moor by wagonette, crossing Tailrigg. There were two sets of beaters, with seven or eight drives a day. In the 1920s, a beater was paid six bob a day, which was reckoned to be good pay. Bill Alderson recalled: "Everybody fell out wi' t'others as to who should go beating." Anyone with a Dales pony could ask for another six bob a day. It had to be a good pony, with a good saddle. Chaps with ponies used to put a collar and tie on to ga' wi' 'em. Gentry didn't want you to go onnyroad..."

Not everyone cared for the taste of grouse. A Swaledale farmer who regularly joined the ranks of the beaters, said: "They mak a hellova shout about it, but to me it's like eating heather. Go and pull a root or two up and thou's about gitten t'same taste. Young grouse don't taste so bad but they [the gamekeepers] give thee old 'uns." On one Dales estate, grouse were hanging in the larder from August to December, then cooked when the landowner came for dinner. "They hanged yon grouse till they dropped off bi t'heads. That's when they were fit to eat. They were bad – but some folk still ate 'em."

In the sunset years of the Edwardian period, Ingleborough Estate, which extended to the gritstone moors further west, paid a gamekeeper £1 a week, plus tied accommodation and a field just big enough to keep a house-cow. The 'keeper might also dig peat as fuel."

The vast moors around Nidderdale were renowned for their grouse and for the employment of a large number of gamekeepers. Major J E E Yorke recalled visiting his grandfather at Bewerley Hall, near Pateley Bridge. On shooting days he travelled by the Nidd Valley light railway to a point where he and his friends might walk on to the moor for some sport. Something of the excitement of grouse-driving on the grand scale was conveyed by W W Tempest, who joined in a penultimate shoot. The beaters, as those who drove the grouse were known, were in the main farmers and farm men who, while it was still dark, had been milking, feeding calves and tending their stock. Each man had then dressed for a long day on the moors and slung across a shoulder a satchel holding food. And each beater carried a large white flag tacked to a stout hazel stick.

At the moor gate, a thousand feet above the village, men squatted in the lee of a limestone wall, smoking and talking while they awaited the arrival of late-comers. "Whya noo, it's nut a bad moornin'," one remarked between long draws at his pipe. The 'keeper explained details of the route to be taken. His listeners nodded politely; they knew the routine of old. A large party set off and it gradually dwindled as men took up their stations. Four men remained when Conny Currack was reached. This was a conical pile of stones erected as a beacon on the summit of this part of the moor. Many such beacons, collectively known as "steean men", were known; they were invaluable to anyone walking in mist or snow.

The shooters, together with gun-loaders and flankers for the drive, had climbed to the moor by another road and were spreading along a line of butts nearly two miles away to the east. From the butts came two shots to indicate that the shooters were ready. The 'keeper sounded a long, strong, high-pitched note on a horn. From another direction, a horn-blower gave a staccato reply. Men sprang to their feet, waving flags, advancing in a broad semi-circle. Scores of grouse rose, fluttering and calling, darkening a bright sky. The beaters shouts of *Brrrr-rr, hay-harrr* mingled with the first reports from the guns. One of the flankers, who was over seventy years old, lay low until the grouse approached, judging the precise moment at which to jump into action. A second too early and the birds would veer away from the guns. A second too late meant they would pass over his head, out of range.

Forty minutes after the start, the beaters arrived at the butts, sweating and ready for a few minutes rest. The "guns" were whistling and calling to their retrievers, who gathered fallen birds. Long before this task was finished, the drivers had formed another line, elsewhere, and were ready to resume the shoot. The weary men then made for the shooting-box and gathered round a peat-burning stove, to eat and to drink steaming hot tea from large jugs that were frequently re-filled. Bottled beer was on hand. A man who had fallen into a hole during the second drive dried his socks on the stove-pipe.

"As the men finish their lunch, the shooters, who have had transport provided, arrive for their repast, which is something more interesting than sandwiches, tea and beer. More horn-blowing. More drives. More shots. Then, at dusk, the drivers, wearied after twenty-five miles of trudging through sodden heather, repair to the domestic fireside or to a local inn." The shooting-boxes varied from wooden huts to single-storey buildings of stone, roofed by slate. But invariably they were divided into two sections – one for the gentry and one for the beaters.

The dalesman acknowledged that grouse "tak a bit o' gettin'. They're not so good to spot and when thou puts 'em up they're not so good to knock down." At the end of the season, he was among the beaters who were offered a day's sport on the moor. "I had ever so many bangs without so much as a feather to show for 'em...I can allus say I've shot at a grouse but I can't truthfully say I've shot one. One day, I got a gurt hare. There were some gentry about at t'time and it was t'biggest hare they'd ever sin. I telled 'em it had better be cos if it had been a lile 'un I'd hev missed it. I didn't know whether to dump it but then I thought, damn, I'll hev to tek it. So I went on beating, carrying yon hare."

In Victorian times, some of the women were better shots than the men and, being more methodical, remembered where the slain birds had fallen. A gun-toting lady on

Burnmoor, near Clapham, was able to recall the whereabouts of up to a score of birds. A man, on the other hand, would comment vaguely to the 'keeper: "I think there's one over there, and another somewhere..." Such a man had not managed to hit a single bird. A sportsman with a non-shooting companion shot one bird then, with the second barrel, another. "Well done, John," shouted his companion, who did not like to admit that the second was not the one he had aimed at.

At a time when life was frugal and brass [money] was in short supply, the onset of grouse-shooting and the need to hire horses and employ farmers and their sons was a welcome boost to the economy, beaters were provided with barrels of beer – "a lot of them nine-galloners" supplied by the nearest hostelry and transported to the moorside by hoss and cart to be distributed among shooting huts associated with the moor. At the end of season, the gamekeeper had to return the empty barrels. He made his helpers put a sheet over the barrels "because he didn't want everybody to know how much had been supped." Some beaters drank so much beer at an intermittent stage that when the later drives took place "they couldn't go so weel and had to lig down. Then t'line o' men was nae good. But nobody ever said owt..."

At lunch-time when, as noted, the nobs resorted to the shooting-hut – "yan room for t'gentry and yan for t'serfs" – hampers of good food were available. At one hut, a farmer's wife provided an appetising tatie pie that was "washed down with *White Horse* whisky and such like." One one minor estate, grouse-shooting was not so much a matter of killing as many birds as you could." It was "a gurt party. Everybody enjoyed thersells. If it was a reight wet day, thou went into t'hut to play cards and drink beer."

At Keasden, Tom Brennand, Dick Townley and a few more were up at t'Back Coppy wi' nowt to drink. "They sent mi fadder, who was then a young lad, up to Middle Hut to get some beer. He wasn't carting beer down so he brought a greeny-coloured bottle [whisky]. He took cork off and necked some. It got down t'wrong hole or summat and he near choked. Old Brennand said: 'Let's hev it.' There were three or four of them. They did that bottle in afore they went."

When a hamper of food fell off the cart and was crushed under the wheels, the driver and his pal picked out what could still be consumed and threw the rest down a banking into t'beck. And when the provisions for the beaters included beef but no bread with which to make sandwiches, they improvised. Their special sandwich was a fatty bit between two pieces of lean beef.

Kettlewell, Wharfedale.

# PART FOUR

# *Autumn*

*As the year declined, and the landscape donned its Jacob's coat of many colours, a hill farmer "laid in" the cattle and made his annual selection of breeding stock. He kept the cows out of doors until the land began to poach [puddle]. Hopefully, this would not happen until November. He resigned himself to twice-a-day milking and mucking-out.*

*Older sheep, their teeth worn down by grazing coarse moorland vegetation, were "drafted" through the auction mart to the low country. The hoggs [lambs of the year] were "salved", a mixture of grease and tar being applied to their skin before October, when they were moved to "lower-down farms". The charge was five shillings each but the change gave young stock a good start in life and relieved grazing pressure on the home acres.*

*Autumn was salving time for all the retained sheep, a salved animal being said to winter better and to be less troubled by insect pests. Old Will Wallbank never got round to salving his sheep. The intention was there but his time was spent melting salve or getting sheep in ready for t'salvers or trying to catch sheep when they were dry.*

*In this busy season, a tup "had its way" with willing ewes. If two rival tups met each other, they would back, then charge, meeting each other head to head with a resounding "clonk". A Sunday School teacher told the touching story of the shepherd who had ninety-nine sheep in the fold but still went out after the missing animal. Why did he do this? A farmer's son said: "Appen t'missing sheep were t'tup."*

*In November, cock grouse were establishing territories and vigorously defending them. Using beak-and-claw, they fought savagely. Hackles were raised and feathers flew. From October onwards, nomadic flocks of fieldfares and redwings, bird immigrants from Scandinavia, filched the vermillion berries from the rowan trees.*

# A TAILOR CALLS

After his evening meal, a farmer donned a smart black jacket over his normal attire and sat beside the kitchen fire. He was being thrifty rather than ostentatious, determined to wear out his wedding suit, which forty years before he had bought from a tailor of quality. Dalesfolk were dress conscious when the need arose, such as if there was an impending funeral and they needed some smart "setting-off" clothes.

A couple living in Upper Wharfedale telephoned a relative at Settle and said they might be called at Dickie Moore's, the outfitters, because one who was "near and dear" was "failing" and might not last long. They had "nowt good to wear" at the funeral. When they did not call within a reasonable time, an explanation was demanded. The reply was: "He got better."

John Haines Wesley Reeson, of Skipton, spent more than thirty years of a busy life visiting customers all over the Craven Dales. Gone were the days when a Dales tailor went from farm to farm, staying overnight so that he might make the required clothes. Reeson, as his full name implied, was a Methodist. He had served in the Great War, returned to the outfitters' business owned by his brother-in-law, whose name was Fielding, and eventually had the business willed to him. His love of travelling in the Dales led him to dispose of the shop. His contemporaries were the aforementioned Dickie Moore of Settle and Alan Aherne of Hellifield.

John Reeson rented a stock room for ten shillings a week and opened the place on Mondays and Saturdays. He was on his Dales rounds on Tuesday, made out the orders on Wednesday and, every fortnight, went to Leeds where the suits for which he had orders were made to measure. He did not have a car, visiting his customers by bus or on foot. He went to a garage intending to buy a car but, having to reverse it out of the place, and not being able to manage it, he cancelled the order and carried on walking.

If business was quiet on Monday, which was market day, John Reeson would rattle the keys in his pocket and tell whoever was around that "I'll just have a walk to t'auction mart and see if there is anyone there." Invariably, he would return with an order. He sold a suit to Mr Falshaw, of Newsholme, as they travelled by train, having told him that suits would be a short supply. Wherever he was, he never forgot that he was a salesman.

A friend was with him on a visit to a farmer where there was an agitated and noisy dog. No-one was at home. As they left, the normally mild-mannered John Reeson picked up a stone and threw it at the dog, remarking: "I've always hated it – but they've always been in." He carried two packs of samples, wrapped in American cloth. He met other tradesmen – grocers, drapers, ironmongers – who were on their rounds. He rarely sold shirts. The daughters of farmers were able to make these at home. If they were to get married, they needed to know how to sew or knit a pair of socks.

Styles were slow to change. For years, the typical suit worn by a Dales farmer was single-breasted, with three buttons, no vent and accompanying waistcoat. He was partial to navy-serges. It was needed for an important event like a wedding. When the next wedding came along, the farmer would get another suit – just the same as before.

When his business was taken over by Henry Cosgrove – "Cos" to his many friends – he bought a car. For a year he was shown the rounds, including a direct route between Malham and Bordley town, a journey that John Reeson had managed quite well on foot. Happily, the conditions were especially dry and the link with Bordley was made. It was a time when the best made-to-measure suits on offer cost £19 but stock sizes of such as Derby tweed were available at £5.

Cos started work on his own account on March 14, 1947, when the dale-country held the cores of snowdrifts from one of the worst winter spells in human memory. When he reached Rainscar, back o' Penyghent, he was told: "You've done very well. The postman hasn't been yet." The car foundered in snow on the steep, zig-zag road from isolated Darnbrook Farm to Arncliffe. It took the efforts of the four Robinson lads from Darnbrook, each with a shovel, to free Cos from a drift.

Those Robinson lads had a gradation of size, the tallest being six foot one inch. Mrs Robinson ordered a suit from time to time for one of the boys or for the husband. Usually, in those pre-electricity days, a suit had gone damp with mildew while hanging upstairs. Cos took his first order for a suit for one of the lads and had it made up. When he delivered it to the farm, it turned out that he had got the wrong set of measurements from John Reeson's book. He had made it for the smallest of the brothers but it was intended for Peter, who was the tallest. He donned it upstairs and returned to the kitchen with his sleeves half-way up his arms and his trousers at half-mast. Cos quickly offered to make a new suit. A customer complained that "these trousers aren't reight. There's one leg shorter than t'other." They were correct. The kitchen floor on which he walked was sloping.

Dalesfolk were good payers but were inclined to settle up when they got the money, such as after a lamb sale. At one call, Cos knew that if the farmer went into the house he might get paid. This man had a rota system. If your name came up, you received the cash. If not, you waited till next time. If he reached for a cardboard box, the tailor definitely knew some cash would be forthcoming.

The farmers' wives were pleased when they were given an out-of-date pattern book. The samples were promptly used up in a pegged rug. Their sense of hospitality led them to provide food for the travelling tailor. He was given breakfast – not long after he had enjoyed breakfast at home. His protestations were swept aside with the words: "Thou's pale. Thou's thin – and thou wants feeding up."

# MAN AND DOG

A shepherd whistled. Over half a mile away, across a wintry tract of moorland, the ears of a collie dog pricked up and it responded to one of four main commands – stop, come on and two flank whistles, instructing the animal to turn left or right. The whistles might vary a little from man to man and from dog to dog when the farmer was "double-dogging". One chap had seven dogs "and none of 'em's on t'same whistle." Yet whistling was better than shouting. A farmer who lost his teeth – and his ability to whistle – carried a small, flat metal whistle he could slip into his mouth as required.

A collie dog is the Artful Dodger of the Moors. The name given to the Dodger had a single syllable – Seth, Bret, Kim – and was shoutable. But the whistle was the prime means of communication between man and dog. "Sometimes, when t'wind's right, you might be working it up to three-quarters of a mile away. I've put mi best dog off on t'top side of an allotment and it's got 'em for me." Sheep got to know the whistles as well as the dog. A farmer who had left his dog at home decided to move some sheep from one pasture to another. He opened the gate, stood beside it and whistled as though a dog was present. The sheep bunched and passed through the gate. "That's not likely to work twice," the man was heard to say. A whistle carried far and was impersonal, unemotional – at least, most times. "Sometimes you got a little excited and put a bit of tension on the dog." Mark Hayton, who farmed on Ilkley Moor, used to say: "Let your dog think and be your servant – not slave...Let the dog teach you, not the other way about." Sam Dyson, who was well-known throughout the Dales as a judge at sheepdog trials, observed: "I talk to my dogs. The more you talk to 'em, the more they learn. When you're training a dog, you want to know when to give ower. And you don't want to come away falling out. If you've fallen out, do something it likes, then call it off and go home as friends."

Without a well-trained dog, the Dales farmer had no hope of managing sheep that were spread over broad upland acres. The visitor to a dalehead farmstead who looked at a local hill observed to the farmer: "I bet you've climbed that hill hundreds of times." He replied: "No – but t'dog has." At times, when snow is in the offing, a quick gather is vital or sheep might be overblown.

A Conistone farmer had a dog for each phase of the work. One was good at gathering sheep and another for driving them home. When he and an old black-and-white tan bitch were shedding [separating] sheep, they passed between him and the dog. With great rapidity, he would say to the dog "come in" or "get out". Instantly, the dog moved in and out, giving the sheep little opportunity to have second thoughts.

The wise farmer kept his eye on a young dog, knowing it could be spoilt if training began when it was not yet ready. Then its small size meant it could not keep up with the sheep. The dog would become disheartened. On the other hand, an animal was likely to turn out badly if it was kept fastened up when it was ready for work. Most dogs were showing an interest in work from the age of five months and would be ready for intensive training when about a year old. The peak of usefulness was reached between the ages of three and six.

Sam Dyson used to say: "The best kind of dog is one that'll stand straightening up and yet when you've finished with it, t'dog'll still be pals with you. If it starts to sulk or owt like that, you get nowhere. Start praising a dog for doing wrong – and it's no good at all." When Sam and his wife Peggy began farming, they had Floss, a brindled collie that had belonged to Peggy's father, who had bought it from a farmer at Bishop Wilton, near York. Floss sneaked off and was shot for sheep-stealing.

"We then bought a little hairy dog. Right hairy face – a little beardy. It cost us five pounds. I brought it home. Chap who sold it to me said: 'Whatever you do, don't let it off t'lead for a week or two or it'll come straight back home. We've sold it before and it allus comes back.' Peggy rubbed its feet wi' butter and left it to lick it off. We let it out on t'morning after and it never went nowhere." The fields were full of sheep – other people's sheep – and "that dog ran those sheep. Wherever they went, it was just there in front of them. Soon we were left with our own stock."

When Sam was young, "I couldn't wait until tea was over and I could get out and laik wi' t'dogs. Nah, when it gets after teatime, I think: 'I wean't bother'. T'fire goes out of it as you get older."

Farmers tended to ignore their dogs when they were not actually working. They consigned them to an outbuilding, never permitted them to enter the house and were enraged if someone actually patted them. The dogs were fed on a diet of flake maize, which was protein deficient, or on any dead animals there happened to be on the farm.

Yet a farmer was tempted to keep a favourite dog well beyond its working age. An old dog that lumbered across the kitchen and rubbed its head against a leg of its master was so accustomed to the route and routine that a stranger would not suspect the dog was – blind.

# SHEEP FOR SALE

A Dales farmer loved to haggle. He managed to do it when chapel-going on Sunday, at a time when he should have had lofty religious thoughts. He had seen some tidy sheep and mentioned to their owner. "If it hadn't bin Sunday, I'd have bid for 'em." Said the owner: "If it hadn't bin Sunday, I'd have bin interested." And so on. A bid was made – and rejected. The price gradually narrowed to one that was mutually acceptable. The transaction was sealed by a handslap. The sheep were collected on the following day.

Haggling was a feature of the local sheep fair, held in the street. Another fair day would see an assembly of tethered cattle. Occasionally a bull broke free and ran amock. One of two brothers who wanted to buy a certain cow, did his best not to seem anxious. The haggling went on interminably. His brother sidled up to him and whispered: "Get it bought, lad. I've just selled it!"

A regular at the sheep fair held on September 27 in the main street at Clapham was Mrs Moore, a dealer from Crooklands. She was regarded as being "a bit mannish" and, when examining a tup, would ask: "What sort of a gitter is he?" Fair Day was bedlam; you couldn't stir all day. "Farmers with bits of hurdles made pens, some of 'em in front of folks's doors. If there were any railings, sheep were tied up agin 'em. Some people couldn't get out of their front doors; there were pens round them and they were fast in."

Buying and selling sheep was thirsty work. At Clapham, the New Inn, run by Harry Boyes, had more ale spilt on t'floor than is drunk today. Local houses were open for refreshments. "You could get as much as you wanted to eat for a shilling." Old Mrs Farrer, carrying her pet Pekingese, made her rounds of the fair. She thought it was great. "No one had t'pluck to remind her that her big house was out o' t'way. When the sheep had gone and the pens were being cleared away, you couldn't see t'ground for sheep muck."

Malham Fair, which flourished before the Great War, was an October event held on the Green. It was a do-it-yourself affair. All was done by barter. A farmer erected his own pen on the same little plot that he claimed year after year. He knew his patch to the yard. "You didn't need much money to buy a sheep. A "shot" lamb sold at from 7s to 10s. A draft ewe made perhaps 15s or 18s. The price rose above £1 only if the animal was summat special. Afterwards, a few old fellows would get into the pub and drink gin. "The farmers took their hurdles home and that was that. Malham Fair was over for another year – except for t'talk about it."

Something of the old-time spirit of the sheep fair was detectable when springtime sheep fairs were inaugurated on a bleak stretch of moor by the Tan Hill inn, which at 1,732 ft was renowned as the highest pub in the land. Its appeal for visitors lay in its informality. There was no formal opening. Ask what time it began, and a farmer might reply: "Hawf past eleven. Summat like that. Or twelve o' clock – summat like." You met the real dalesfolk, including Aldersons and Raines, Harkers and Calverts.

Swaledale sheep, fretful at being penned and inclined to butt each other if no one was looking, were judged by respected flockmasters. They scrutinised "head, carcass, coat". The coat [fleece] must be good enough to stand up to a Pennine winter. It should have depth and be a little curly on top. If it was too fine, and there came a spell o' bad weather, it might shed [part] and the sheep'd be starved." The tups looked magnificent, as well they might. A grizzle-grey farmer, still keen on sheep though no longer keeping any, was heard to comment: "This lot will have been wintered in t'parlour. It's sheep out theer [the moor] that are t'yardstick."

In the hostelry, a farmer extended a brief greeting to a

friend: "How ista?" "Nobbut living". "Haven't seen you all winter; thought you'd passed on." "I'se bin deeard a lang while; I'se too idle to stiffen." They laughed. The first man said: "Then let's be celebrating." "Aye, if thou's paying for it." A more serious conversation had developed in the far corner of the bar. "We lost t'lamb o'yon ewe." "Deeard?" "Aye, 'appen brozzen [sated] itsen wi' milk... It wor a reight bonnie 'un, too."

When the auction mart took the place of the sheep sale, transactions were regularised and the event took on more of a social context. On a day when a man was freed of farmyard duties, he might relax with his friends and, later, over a pint of ale at a local hostelry. One market-fresh farmer staggered into yet another pub, leaving his horse and trap standing in the yard. Some local lads took the horse out of the shafts, turned it round and re-harnessed it, so that when the bleary-eyed owner next saw it he drawled: "I nivver thowt I'd see a hoss kick a trap ower its heeard."

## THE SALVERS

Applying a mixture of grease and tar to the skin of sheep was a smelly, irksome, protracted job. You might spend an hour on one animal. The season for hand-shedding and salving was October and early November, being immediately followed by tupping-time. Salvers tended to be anti-social for a while, being conspicuous by having black hands. The hands of a Littondale man who was married at salving time contrasted markedly with those of his bride as he slipped the ring on her finger.

A salver shared a stock [wooden bench] with the sheep. The salve was handy, a quantity being put in a wooden bowl that had a long handle which fitted into a hole on the stock. The wool was systematically parted, or shedded, and a salver usually "striped" the salve, collecting some on a finger and running the finger along the bared skin in a single movement. He would then shed another length of wool.

Norman Swindlehurst, who salved sheep prior to the 1914-18 war, said the task lasted for about a month. "We hadn't many sheep. We lambed sixty. A grease called Black Jack and a brown salve were bought from a man called Sedgwick, who travelled through the district from his home at Sedbergh. The Black Jack arrived at Clapham station in tubs and the farmers had it to cart up."

The Irvings of Skipton, who made up salve for sale, began the mixing process in late summer, when two or three men set to work to warm up and blend the ingredients in huge set-pots, ready for the big rush of orders in September and October. With salve, much depended on the air temperature. Archangel tar was quite a stiff tar whereas Stockholm tar, derived from wood, was easier to use.

Grease in the salve helped the sheep to shed rainwater, though gave any wool that came into contact with it indelible marks. The tar was used for sheep-scab, which an old-time writer described as "a grievous offensive disorder or sorrance among sheep, especially those much exposed to rainy weather or great mists or fogs; over-driven much in wet dirty ways." Tar also killed the lile flat lice known to the farmers as kades. Even so, you were "terribly bothered with these kades". Too much tar and "you burnt your wool". It was wise to add a bit o' milk to the tar "to tak t'sting oot of it." Robert Wallbank, of Keasden, went to Liverpool to buy tar at the docks. They were consigned to Clapham by train. Robert kept some tar for himself and sold the rest off to other local farmers. You could buy either black tar (which stained your hands badly) or white tar. It was considered that white tar was better at "turning the weather". The grease was in the form of whale-oil or cheap butter [sixpence a pound].

The salve, being smelly and inflammable, was made outdoors, using a sort of fireplace put together with bricks. On it reposed a big iron pan. When the grease had melted, the tar was added.

The proportions were two-thirds of grease to one of tar. A big stick was used for stirring the salve, which smelt abominably as it melted – it was not boiled – and then the salve was poured into a tub. The iron pan was now available for making another lot. At one of the larger farms, seven or eight tubs of salve would be required.

Salving began with the hoggs which, at the beginning of October, were moved to lower ground for a winter holiday. "Then we started on t'ewes." Good weather was essential. No salving could take place if fleeces were wet. "There was a knack in catching sheep dry". The salvers included old men who went from farm to farm. William Atkinson, nicknamed Ditheram, was not paid money but received from the farmer a new shirt and a pair of fustian trousers. Other veterans were Alf Leek, who was called Opplefrog, and William Thornborough, whose nickname, Mowdy, indicated that at other times he went in pursuit of moles. They didn't come from anywhere; they just roamed t'country, getting a job here and there. But they'd always turn up at salving time. The hands of the Black Hand Gang had returned to their natural pink a few weeks after the salving operation ended.

At a big farm like Keasden Head, "there'd be into t'teens of 'em salving." Farmers tended to help each other, as with sheep-clipping. They would start in good time in the morning and work until ten o'clock at night. They worked in t'shippons and calf-holes. At night they just had lanterns with a candle in and some had candles stuck in a bit of wood. "You got all shut up with some sheep and it got warm." At times the smell was so dense and odious it made a salver sick. "Then we had to oppen t'door and let a bit more air in."

As you only wanted one sheep an hour, you caught your own. It was expecting too much of sheep to be quiet for the whole hour. "Sometimes they frigged. They never gave in. They were determined to t'finish." A restless sheep might have its legs tied to incapacitate it but this was not a general practice. When we were doing right down t'middle o' t'back, we put the legs between t'bars on t'stock.

Drink was provided, but at one farm, where home-brewed ale was "poor washy stuff", the men concluded "you were as well drinking tea." There was always fun and tale-telling. There were some good tales and some black 'uns – we heard all sorts. When salving ended, there was "all t'mook [muck] to clane oop after." When dipping was compulsory, salving was practised on a limited scale. A prosecution for salving instead of dipping took place in 1906 and the farmer was fined. (A few farmers with old-time views were salving in the 1930s. They preferred this irksome job to using arsenical dips).

## TUPPING TIME

The Dales new year began with a crack as two rival tups met head to head when a footloose animal came up with one that was in the company of its harem of about fifty willing ewes. A fight between rival males could be fearsome with each animal backing, then charging. It was often the smallest tup that prevailed, its head catching the other's nose. A farmer who tried to intervene had a finger so badly crushed it had to be amputated.

Prized tups were given the best of food the winter through. A visitor to Cam Houses, the remote group of farmsteads near the headwaters of the Wharfe, discovered that the Lamberts kept their most prized tups in the front room. Summer was spent languishing on good pastureland. Now, with shortening days, the tups became restless.

Just when the tups were released depended on a farmer's

assessment of grass-growth in the following spring but it would be sometime in April, allowing for a gestation period of 147 days. "Start thee tupping on Guy Fawkes' day – and thou should hev summat to show for it on All Fools' Day." If a farm was at the dalehead, a later date would be fixed. The best-laid plans could be ruined by a footloose tup belonging to a neighbour.

A tup was used for two years – "that autumn, then the next autumn" – and by t'next year, when it was "going to mate with its own stock", it was sold or swapped.

In the days before fine breeding of specific types, a Keasden farmer used "cross-bred 'uns, what was called 'country bred' – a bit of all-sorts." He once bought some Rough Fell sheep from Sedbergh and Kendal. "That sharpened 'em up." Despite the long experience of farmers in selecting appropriate stock, mistakes were made. "I yance hed a tup and they all lambed in a fortneet. And another time, wi' different tup, about half of t'yows were gelt [sterile] and I had to get another."

The finest tups for hill stock were sold at the October sales in Hawes and Kirkby Stephen. A Keasden farmer who decided to go to the tup sale at Kirkby Stephen entrained at Clapham, left the train at Giggleswick, and walked across the valley to catch a train from Settle. At Kirkby Stephen, there was a mile and a-half walk into town. Then, on the return, he faced the long, steep walk upbank to the railway and an especially tiring reversal of the outward journey. "You could lead a tup best if you had a rope round its horns and another round the back of t'front legs and took hold of that. It was like a handle."

The Midland Railway put extra vans on local trains at sale time. The tup was tied up in a van. By the time man and tup, having reached Clapham station, had undertaken the long slog up the moor road, both were tired. One or two tups got lost. "A man'ud get on t'spree [pub crawl] and forget what he should be doing."

# A QUARRY COMMUNITY

Quarries pockmarked every fellside. Living rock was painstakingly separated from ancient beds to be used for buildings. Scree and outcrop were formed into a futuristic pattern of drystone walls. The many quarrymen working in the Dales also managed to export stone, as from Burtersett, in Wensleydale, which throve between the 1860s and the Great War and had trade links with Lancashire. Stone was transported on two-horse wagons to Hawes railway station, to be consigned to the developing cotton towns. Flagstones were cut for the streets of big cities, including London.

Horses used for haulage work were of the Shire type, which was large and hefty. Most of them had been bought at special fairs, one of which was held on Askrigg Hill in early July and at Brough Hill at the end of September. One year, at Askrigg Hill fair, Kit Fothergill came to the rescue of an old chap sent by the quarry to sell a horse. He had been defrauded by a dealer and lost both the horse and the money. Kit traced the horse to Wibsey Fair, at Bradford, where he also saw two other Wensleydale horses that had been lost in suspicious circumstances. The dealers bolted.

The type of stone-wagon hauled by the horses was four-wheeled, the front wheels being on a turntable. There were shallow sides. Loading a wagon took place from a ramp and quarrymen were clever at swinging a stone that was held vertically so that with minimum effort they could move it where they wished. On the descent of the hill from Burtersett, the carter jammed a wheel with a "slipper", a wooden wedge attached by chain to the cart. It made a prominent groove in the road – much to the chagrin of the local council surveyor, who instructed his men to fill in the channel.

Quarrying was desperate work. Workers rarely suffered from the lung troubles that afflicted the lead-miners of the district, some of whom – Peacocks, Pratts and Reynoldsons – switched occupations, preferring the subterranean world in Quarry Hill, aglow with the light of tallow candles, to the constrictions of the Swaledale mines.

At Burtersett two rival commercial enterprises had been built up by Dicky and Tom (yet more members of the huge Metcalfe clan). Competition between them was keen. The operation of removing stone for flags and buildings was really a cross between quarrying and mining. The best rock came from drifts that penetrated the hillside for anything up to half a mile, pillars being left to support the roof. No explosives could be used. The men operated hand-drills. Pony-drawn trucks brought out the stone. At a blacksmith's shop, tools were sharpened and new shoes provided for the wagon horses. The dressers, who worked in a large shed, took tea in bottles for their mid-day break and left the bottles beside the smithy fire to be kept warm. Underground workers – those "up t'hole" – drank their tea cold. Down the drift they could at least cheat the bitter Pennine weather.

Working hours were from 7-30 until 4 p.m., with half an hour off for dinner. The men worked for six days and they had only two days of holiday, these being Good Friday and Christmas Day. One man who worked at Burtersett quarry for sixteen years had one week off – the period following his marriage in 1902. When, in due course, his joints stiffened and his capacity for work was impaired, he had his wage reduced from 18s to 16s a week. Later on, crippled with rheumatism, he had to give up work altogether. There was no leaving present. Subsequently, he earned a pittance breaking up stone for the local council. He also swept the village roads, along which moved the horse-drawn wagons bearing stone from Burtersett quarry to Hawes station. For this work he was given £3 a year.

Burtersett was a quarry community, made up of large families. A dozen people managed to fit themselves into a two-bedroom house. There were two other houses of this size, each with a large family - and a few lodgers, young men, looking for work. Some of them left seeking better wages when a forceful Irishman, John Delaney, began to develop his limestone quarries in North Ribblesdale and Upper Wharfedale.

Despite poor wages and grim working conditions, the oldest workers lived for the quarry. Their lives were divided between bed and work. A rheumaticky old man walked from Hardraw to Burtersett each working day, arriving on the Hill in time to commence work at 7-30 a.m. He was never late, in winter or summer. In a lifetime of service to the quarry, his weekly wage never exceeded sixteen shillings.

Quarrymen were apt to find spare time boring. Few of them darkened the doors of the local Methodist and Congregational chapels. On Sunday, when there was no work, more than one quarryman stayed in bed until well into the morning, rose, pottered about, had dinner and then, quite often, return to bed in the afternoon until their wives shouted: "Tea's ready."

Amonghands, they tended geese and hens. When hen eggs cost as much as a penny each, the family did not eat any. The eggs must be sold. "When eggs were sixteen for a shilling, we could have one now and again. And when eggs were being sold at eighteen or twenty for a shilling, mother put them down into waterglass and used them for baking during the winter."

In those hard times, each child received a Tuesday halfpenny. It was a stigma on a family if the money could not be raised. Kit Calvert recalled: "Down at Hawes, on our way to school, we called at Old Tommy Metcalfe's (we called him Tommy Spiffs) and Mrs Metcalfe stood waiting with a lot of boxes of sweets. We rooted among 'em. She had a church magazine beside her and every time someone picked anything, she tore a page out of the magazine and made a cone of it to hold the sweets."

Wensley Church.

*PART FIVE*

# *T'Back End*

*To step outside the house at night was to walk under an arc of stars or into darkness. Pin-pricks of light indicated where other farmsteads lay. It was quiet except for the occasional barking of a farm dog. In winter, dalehead families seem to grow an extra skin. A housewife kept warm through hard work. Going to bed was a cheerless experience. The temperature in an unheated bedroom remained low. The oilcloth that covered the floor was chilling to the foot, except where it was covered by a pegged-rug. Frost-pictures appeared on bedroom windows overnight.*

*A farmer, attending to an outside job, seemed impervious to the bitter air and was inclined to refer to a gale as "a bit of a blow." Cattle were let out of their quarters, usually two at a time, to drink at the well in the yard. If the well was frozen over, the farmer took a hammer and broke the ice. On a sunny morning, it was not easy to persuade the cows to return; they would run around the outbarn, ignoring the door to the byre.*

*When the air filled with flakes of snow, children recited "They're pluckin' geese in Scotland and sending feathers here." At other times, the frosty air had the tingle factor. A dozen eager draughts seeped into the farmsteads and kept people within easy range of the fire.*

*Just before Christmas, a flurry of work saw the grim and messy task of pig-killing. Plucking geese left the hands raw and clothes flecked with goose-down. It was goose, rather than turkey, that graced the table on Christmas Day. Much of the grease was poured into jars to be rubbed on the chests of ailing children. "Tha could use goose-grease on thi clogs, especially through t'lace holes. It stopped watter getting in."*

# THE DALESMAN'S COW

In winter, the smell of cows pervaded all, especially at a longhouse, where farmhouse, barn and shippon were under one capacious roof. After tea, a farmer slurred his chair on the flagged floor and rose to announce that he was "bahn to milk". On a dalehead farm, the shippon might have tying for a dozen cows. Hay was transferred to the booses from the mewstead via the foddergang. As a cow ate, the farmer, sitting on his traditional three-legged stool, with his cap turned so the neb was at the back and a pail between his legs, coaxed milk from heavy teats.

A Shorthorn, which was not short-papped, was a good cow to milk. And it actually waited for him to begin work. He'd had a cow that "started sprayin' out milk as soon as it heard t'proven bucket". In that gloomy, cobwebby, sickly sweet-smelling building one heard little more than the rustle of hay, the hiss of a paraffin lamp, the swish of milk against the side of the pail and the slap, slap, slap of cow-claps in the making. After milking, mucking-out began…

New-calved cows were kept near the farm and fed large quantities of oatmeal gruel, into which some linseed might be mixed to give them "a bit o' heat". A calf was so valuable that a Swaledale farmer habitually sat up with a cow for a week before she dropped her calf. Widespread interest was shown in the calves. "What 'ev you gitten?" "Oh, it's a great span [red and white] bull calf." A "wie" calf was white. A cow would drop a "grand roan wie cawf – it's a bezzler."

A farmer dreaded the day when a cow aborted its calf or showed symptoms of John's disease, "a desperate thing". Milk fever was cured by pumping oxygen into the cow's bag. (Ugh!). Linseed oil or castor oil was used when there was a "stoppage". Ringworm was overspread with a mixture of engine oil and black sulphur. Or collop [bacon] fat and brimstine – wi' a bit o' turpentine. "Nivver known it to fail."

Shorthorn milk, with a high percentage of butter-fat, made good butter and cheese. "When you put milk in bowls, to separate the cream, you knew it was ready when the cream would 'od a penny.

It was customary to milk cattle out-of-doors and transport the milk to the farmhouse in a back-can. When not in use, the milking stool was placed in a tree "where it wouldn't get wet and mucky." The cows were frisky early in the season and a dog was needed to round them up. Then they fell into the milking routine and knew their places. A handful of special feed in a bucket encouraged them to drop their milk. The milker, having attended to one cow, would turn to see another, standing patiently, "watchin' t'bucket, wi' slather running over her chin."

The Shorthorn cow was thrifty; it would give milk without a lot of keep and also had a long, productive life. Kit Calvert, who bought a useful little cow for £14.5s during a depression period, kept her for five years, then – on quitting farming – left the cow with his brother Bob. She continued to have calves. Bob eventually considered that the "old lady" was finished; she had not wintered well but was holding another calf. He took her to the mart, feeling "shamed" because the cow looked so run-down. A dealer looking for some cheap stock snapped her up.

Jobbers had toured the dale-country, buying up surplus stock. Their job was supplanted by the auction mart. When Bill Alderson was a lad, he led a new-calved cow from the family farm at Angram in Swaledale part way to the auction mart at Hawes. "I went as far as the Parting Liberties, on t'Buttertubs [pass]. This was the boundary between Swaledale and Wensleydale. Father, setting off later on horseback, met me and went on with the cow. I rode the horse home. He sold his cow at Hawes mart, stayed in town overnight and walked back the next day."

Kitty Hutchinson was "a niggardly old boy" who steadfastly refused to give luck [a small coin marking the completion of a deal]. When a cattle dealer called Willie Fell inquired about luck in advance of a sale, he was told by Kitty that if he bought the beast he would be twice lucky. And so it was. Kitty wished him luck – then gave him a shilling.

Many young in-calf cows were bought by the cow-keepers of Liverpool, who were closely related to farming families living in the upper dales. (The Liverpool comedian Tommy Handley, of ITMA fame, had a Dales ancestry, his family hailing from Garsdale). The cow-keepers supplied milk to householders in a burgeoning city. Cattle intended for Liverpool "must look as though they would give a canny drop o' milk, with good artificial feeding." When a cow finished its time in the city, it was taken to an abbatoir and its replacement was usually found at a Dales mart.

As the milk demand increased, the Dales-type Shorthorn got a "smittlin'" of other breeds, especially the Ayrshire. Some farmers were "not particular about type o' bull they used" and the quality of the old stock declined. Buying a bull was always a chancy operation unless the farmer went to a dealer who had a good name. Few farms trusted a bull and with good cause. Each year one or two dale-farmers were injured or gored when what had seemed to be a docile animal turned on them. August was a particularly unreliable month. It was then that a bull "maks a terrible noise and sends t'sods flying."

Dales farmers did not keep their cattle too long. Many parted with them when they had their third or fourth calf. You might conceal the age of a cow by removing some of the rings that formed on the horns with the passing years. Bill Alderson said: "They didn't do much o' that in Swaledale: but in some parts they kept cows to all ages and some might have twelve calves. T'farmers would file, file, file at the horn to take the wrinkles out. They would have been done today for jiggery-pokery!"

To tour a farm with a herd of old-style Shorthorns was a memorable experience in late summer before stock was being de-horned and the black-and-white Friesian was becoming popular. It gave more milk than a Shorthorn. In the early days, the quality was suspect. "I calls it a watter-can." In former times there was a pleasing dispersal of stock. Youngsters occupied a large pasture near the house. In another field lay the milk cows, their horns upsweeping, turning in gracefully at the top. The next field held a few dried-off cows and beyond was a field of bullocks. In the last good field before the moor were the in-calf heifers and stirks.

Old Shorthorns never seemed to die – they were sold to someone just before they expired.

## VILLAGE HOPS

The annual Christmas dance, known to many as t'Kersmass Hop, was so lively and so crowded that everyone became bathed in sweat. At one village, an old chap who was an excellent fiddler had a weakness for drink. He did not begin to play until he had received a glass of ale. He sipped it between every dance. Given enough ale, he'd play almost non-stop throughout the night. By the time the dance was drawing to a close, he was almost out of the world but ale seemed to put life into his tunes. His legs became so wobbly, he fell and, being picked up, was dumped in an old corn bin to keep him upright.

Old Will Wallbank, who lived at Keasden Head, walked over the fell into Tatham and danced all night. He had a lantern with a bit o' candle in it. As he came back, he passed one or two of the outbarns and stopped off to feed the cattle for folk who could stay in bed for so much longer. George Robinson, wearing newly-greased clogs, walked from

Catlow Farm, at the head of the Hodder valley, using a moorland trod, to the shooting box on the Keasden side of the hill. The hut was locked. When he changed from clogs to shoes, he left his clogs under the shooting hut and walking on to Rantree Farm, where he met up with a pal. Together, in shoes, they attended a dance at the Temperance Hall. The dance ended in the early hours. They returned on foot to Rantree for "t'bit o'neet that was left". Once, when George returned to the shooting hut for his clogs, he found that mice had eaten the leather "uppers".

Thomas Airton was a farmer who would sooner play his fiddle at dances than work on the land. In his day, dances were held in the living rooms of larger farmhouses. "At latter end of a dance, Tom'd fair warmed 'em up." A Shepherds' Ball was a hardy annual event at Wood Gill, Keasden. "It was a good dance and there was any amount to eat. They cleared all the furniture from t'living room. "Over thirty of us danced on a flag floor. Not everybody could get up at once. You took it in turn to dance. Them 'at didn't care for dancing crossed to t'old house and played cards."

At a Conservative Ball in the Three Peaks Country, two farmer's sons had a wager as to who could join in most dances. "We danced every dance, from eight o' clock till three, and never had any supper. I was trying to do a Highland Fling at t'finish and mi feet wouldn't come off t'ground. I set off to walk home and, reaching a bridge, I sat on it. I was tired. I set off again, then got down at roadside and went to sleep. When I wakened up, it was daylight. I was near starved to death [chilled]."

# A HIDDEN DALE

Bell Pratt was born at Round Ing, a farm at the head of Grisedale, a valley tucked away out of sight of the world at the head of Garsdale. When he was a lad, Grisedale had eight active farms and was occupied by familes with dale-country names – Lund, Allen, Thwaite, Harper and, of course, Pratt. Such little farms were just viable. "We made a living, not a fortune." The income came mainly from sheep.

By being christened Bell Pratt, use was made of two surnames, in the old Dales manner. He had the same name as his father, who came to farm in Mallerstang. His mother, Elizabeth Metcalfe, was born in Swaledale. At Round Ing, they reared seven children, five sons and two daughters, and as was the case with most young people, within a short distance of leaving school they went into farm service.

The valley held small herds of Shorthorn cattle and 120 Swaledale-type sheep that went on to the open fell. Round Ing was never a large farm, having about forty acres of inside land. "We milked three, sometimes four cows, had a weekly churning to make butter, fed spare milk to the calves and kept a few hens. Just after the Great War, Bell Pratt's father bought another piece of land, about twenty acres, and the two were farmed together.

From Round Ing, you could see the trains arriving at and departing from Garsdale station. "So at haytime you did not need a clock or a watch in your pocket. Though your tummy would tell you when it was dinner or teatime, you could also work out the time from the appearance of regular trains. After school, he was doing full-time farm work. "We cut peat on the fell beyond the farm and in about September we'd take a horse and cart to Garsdale station for coal. We went to the station, helped ourselves to what was in a wagon, then went down to the bottom of the hill where there was a weighbridge and paid for what you had taken." Garsdale station was the place to visit if livestock or parcels were expected and, twice a year, to make a train journey to Hawes as a treat. Such a trip was made on Whit Tuesday and on the day of Hawes Fair, which took place at the end of September.

At clipping time, Bell's task, as the youngest and therefore the most active person, was to catch the sheep and deal with the fleeces. Male lambs and the older ewes were sold off in the autumn. Any surplus butter was taken to William Hodgson Harper's little shop at Garsdale Head – a shop where you could buy almost anything, even feeding stuffs for cattle. Mr Harper presided over his shop for over fifty years.

Some of Bell's relations were cattle dealers. Father's uncle, William Pratt, who lived at Clough View, was a dealer and also a Methodist local preacher. The Pratt family, who were equally well-known at Oban mart, purchased Highland cattle and sheep. "The Highland cattle they brought to the area had great big horns. This stock did well on the rich pastures of the Yorkshire Dales."

## SONGS OF PRAISE

The approach of Christmas was as delectable to the isolated families as Christmas itself. At the chapel, carols were rendered by lusty voices and without reference to the hymn book. The aforementioned Grisedale was a God-fearing valley. Nothing disturbed the Sabbatical hush except activities at the chapel, where voices were raised in lusty prayers and lively hymn-singing. "On a fine Sunday, everybody went to chapel – except one man. He went on special occasions, such as Christmas."

Going to chapel was not an irksome job in a remote area where there were few distractions from everyday work. Grisedale chapel, built in 1889, commemorated Richard Atkinson, a gamekeeper who became an evangelist of renown. There was seating for about forty worshippers. They sat for long periods on pitch-pine seats. In the early days, when there was no organ, Will Lund "raised the tunes." On the first Sunday in July, a time when the smell of new-mown hay hung in the air above Grisedale, a camp meeting was held outdoors. Those taking the lead stood on a borrowed cart and the worshippers sat on forms. In the evening a Love Feast took place. The feasting was mainly spiritual. All that was handed round was a Loving Cup containing water and some biscuits. It was a time for the people to testify about the effect God's love had on them.

A Nonconformist chapel was both a place of worship and a community centre – vital where families were widely scattered. They needed a focal point. An isolated Methodist chapel such as the one at Widdale Foot or Garsdale Head was in the handiest position for a widely scattered group of farms. Worshippers almost shook the rafters with the singing of mighty hymns. They responded with fervent "amens" to the fiery appeal of local preachers – pulpit-thumpers who confirmed your fears, embellished your hopes and had a no-holds-barred attitude towards Sin. At Grassington, it is said, a woman, much moved by the preacher's appeal to be "saved", stood up and said: "O Lord, tak my lad by his clogs and dangle him ower hell's fire." Then, remembering that the clogs were new, she added: "But nobbut give him a swither."

An excited preacher shouted and waved his arms with such force a small boy turned to his Grannie and asked: "What would happen if he got out?" They had extempore prayers that were inclined to be repetitive. A young preacher "on note" was accompanied to his first solo appointment by an experienced preacher who would later report on the way he conducted the service. The main criticism was the prayer. "Did ta read it?" the old man asked. The young man nodded. "Nay, lad," said his spiritual guide, "prayers should come from the heart, not from a lile bit o' paper."

Margaret Batty, who ministered at Reeth, in Swaledale, related that when much of the original preaching was by itinerants they never forgot their times in the Dales Circuit. It was notorious for "unspeakable weather, damp beds and people so hardened that they never noticed either." They were among an independent, self-reliant folk who appreciated plain speaking. Before chapels were built, they met in each other's homes. At Mill Dam, tucked away in a fold of the hills above Bentham, the spirit of early Dales Methodism was sustained. Forms were carried from an outbuilding and set down in the parlour. The pulpit was a rostrum slipped over the back of a chair. The window framed a view of Ingleborough.

Methodism began in song and chapel folk enjoyed a good sing, especially to a familiar tune. The harmonium, described by a Methodist minister as "an ill wind that nobody blows any good", wheezed and wailed if not properly used. A preacher who heard unfamiliar strains from a harmonium, said to the lady organist: "Can we have a more up-to-date tune?" She replied: "You can't have anything more up-to-date than this. I'm makkin' it up as I go on."

A preacher was to remember Barden, in Wharfedale, for the lunch that followed the service. It was provided by the lady chapel-keeper, who lived in the house on the ground floor. She was also the organist – and, on this occasion, one of a congregation of two. As she passed the pulpit on her way to the organ, she whispered: "Cut thi sermon short when thou smells t'Yorksher pudding."

At a chapel where the preacher found one old chap, he said: "Let us have a few words of prayer and go home." "Nay," said his listener, a retired farmer, "if I had a cow in t'outbarn I'd go and fodder it." The preacher prayed for half an hour, preached for three-quarters of an hour and had four hymns. When he had pronounced the Benediction, the old man rose stiffly to his legs and said: "If I'd getten a cow at t'outbarn, I wouldn't give it all t'hay at once."

## PORK AND POULTRY

The best bacon came from a pig that had celebrated a birthday [it was over a year old]. Pig-killing was a gory business. Anyone brought up on a farm could never forget the squeals of the distraught pig as it was held before being knocked down with a felling-axe, which was a big spike on a long shaft. "You swung it back and hit t'pig on t'forehead. One chap had three go's at a pig with a so-called humane killer and each time t'pig got off t'stock." A dead pig could retaliate. After it was dead, there might be nervous spasms. A dead animal was being moved up t'yard to a building where it would be dressed when "one leg lashed out and hit an old chap on the shin; he had to go and sit down and wasn't able to do any more work."

The pig-killer put the animal on a stock, as used for sheep-shearing. At one farm, a stock collapsed, so another was brought, with the same consequence. The frantic farmer dashed into the house, dragged out the sofa and laid the pig on that. The slaughterer returned a day or so later to cut up the pig. An apprentice made such a bad job of cleaving the suspended body of a pig that his boss said: "Go easy, lad – or thou'll hev both lugs [ears] on one side."

Ham that had been hanging from a hook in the ceiling for a year had acquired a good flavour. Bacon was a staple, eaten at most meals. An average family consumed two pigs a year. In the days when families were truly neighbours, one family – having had a pig killed – would have a surfeit of pork, some of which was distributed. The same applied at other farms. "By swapping back'ard and forrard, you had fresh pork nearly all t'time."

Old Mrs Close, of Dovenanter, made sure she got the most out of the Christmas pig. In a process she called "finishing it off", she trapped it against a wall, sitting on its rump. The pig was then force-fed with oatmeal balls and given "a sup o' milk" now and again. A fatty animal was popular. Bacon were nowt if, when you ate it, fat didn't dribble from each side of your mouth. Pig's trotters were tasty if cut off a foot above t'hock, which meant that what you got had a leg attached. When cooked and set out on a plate, they were tackled using the fingers, not a fork. "Your fingers and mouth got sticky. If you'd never tried one, you'd soon be asking for another." A few people made pig-tripe, emptying the stomach, scraping it and allowing it to remain in salt water for a day or two. "Then you could scrape all t'inside o' t'belly off before boiling it.".

At a farm on Malham Moor, surplus "porkers", aged about eight weeks, were taken to market and sold. Pigs retained for home consumption were reared on "blue milk", a by-product of the butter-making process, also pig-meal and bran. A drop o' milk put a fair shine on their skins. Pig-meat was salted, bought in block-form from a dealer and crunched up by the deft use of a rolling pin. Salting took place on naked benks or surplus "leads", the trays used for settling milk. A layer of salt was put in the lead, and then the shoulders and hams were laid, with the flitch on top, for it must not become too salty. A little salt petre was rubbed around the bone. Too much salt petre made the meat red and rather hard. A layer of salt completed the operation. "Flies would not trouble it; they didn't like salt."

The salted pork, hung from hooks driven into beams in the kitchen, was a hazard to visitors who rubbed against it. A man who did so when wearing his blue "chapel suit" was left with conspicuous greasy marks. Seven pieces of pork were to be seen, these being two hams (that had been left in a salt solution for a month), two shoulders (about three weeks), two flitches (around ten days) and the cheeks (a week).

Just prior to Christmas, the goose flock was culled and the birds were plucked and dressed for the market. Neighbours shared the task of plucking – and through ceaseless chatter, caught up with the latest gossip. Herbert and Julia Haythornthwaite, brother and sister, reared lots of geese, keeping one of them under the kitchen table, where it had food scraps thrown to it by the diners. At Burtersett, in upper Wensleydale, cottagers kept broody geese indoors. The goslings were sold and money apportioned to buying new suits for the lads to wear at chapel on Whit Sunday. A goose that pecked a visitor was whacked with a stick and rendered infertile. That year, there were no new suits for the lads to wear.

A farmer's wife supplied geese to a butcher in the market town of Settle. Each bird was valued at 7s.6d. Rather than settling up, the butcher paid in small sums, which meant that the lady had many a journey into town seeking "a bit o' goose money." Such a journey involved a train journey from Clapham to Giggleswick and a connecting horse bus into Settle. If the butcher paid her in gold and she returned home with as little as half a sovereign, she ruefully calculated that she had almost spent it on fares.

"There always had to be a jar of goose-grease about to treat anyone with whooping cough or bad coughs in winter." The breast feathers of geese and ducks were kept for stuffing into mattresses and cushions. "We used to 'stove' them. We had no boiler and so we took them to a neighbour who had and had a full day 'stoving' feathers. A fire was lit under the boiler and the feathers tipped in to be stirred until 'that soft bit at t'end o' t'feathers' had been dried up." Then they could be kept for a long time. When the first lot of feathers had been bagged, a second lot was processed, and so on. Feathers were fed into a calico mattress cover through a small hole. It was a tedious process for as some feathers were pushed into the mattress others already in place were inclined to drift out.

## CHRISTMAS

The festive season, a bright period in a drab winter, lacked trimmings. One essential feature was a Nativity play performed by schoolchildren. Ella Pontefract, in 1939, recorded a play performed at Halton Gill in Littondale, where one small angel was "a chubby, rosy cheeked child with a beam of joy and goodwill on his face. We met him another day shouting in far from gentle language to an obstreperous cow." A schoolteacher gave an account of the Nativity and of how there was no room at the inn. One of a group of seven year olds said: "I blame Joseph – he should have booked."

Old men believed the cattle in the byre knelt down on Christmas morning in honour of the Christ Child. The children awoke to find stockings holding a few nuts, an orange and perhaps a sugar mouse with a tail made of wool. Not every family had a Christmas tree. At one farm, a small conifer was felled on Christmas Eve and was festooned with candles and other decorations. The farmer and his wife went to milk. A child ran out and said the tree had caught fire. One of the children had applied a match to a candle, which fell over. The child added: "We put it out – with a jug of milk." Christmas was to be remembered for an all-pervading smell of burnt milk.

Christmas Day was just another working day at a farm in upper Baldersdale. This valley began in the temperate zone of Teesdale and ended in the shadow of lean Pennine ridges which, at Christmas, had a crust of snow and ice. Hannah Hawkswell lived alone at Low Birk Hatt, which stood, open to all the winds that blow, at an elevation of nine hundred feet.

She was solitary but not lonely, for there were friends in the local families. She also had a dog named Chip, two cats and a few cattle around which her daily round, seven days a week, was organised. When I met her in 1979, she told me that during the week before the previous Christmas she tied up the cattle in the byres and resigned herself to the extra work this would involve. Hannah both loved and hated her cattle. She most certainly liked them but was sometimes weary of the demands they made on her time and energy. This was her fiftieth winter at Low Birk Hatt, to which she moved with the family when she was a small child. One by one, the members of the family died, leaving Hannah to cope as best she could.

Hannah disliked winter. As gales pounded her house, loosening yet more slates, she dreamt about what she imagined the Mediterranean to be like – a blue sea under a blue sky. Winter in upper Balderdale saw snowdrifts arching themselves against the buildings. Sometimes the wind whirled the snow in an action the dalesfolk called "stouring". The previous winter had been the worst she could remember. Some of the walls that were gapped by the freeze-thaw process remained gapped.

Winter overlapped spring. The summer seemed pitifully brief, with the days apparently rushing towards another winter. "Only the weeds seem to thrive," said Hannah. "Its amazing how they recover after a bad winter." No one had called on Christmas Day, though she had a visitor on Boxing Day. "I'm not really a Christmassy person now," said Hannah. She was absorbed by "beast work". As she reflected on the colder end of the year, she observed wistfully: "I wish it was always summer."

# LAST RITES

A dalesman did not die – he was takken. A Methodist "crossed Jordan" or went to "his reward." Some were takken quick and others lingered. It was said of a man who had reached the age of ninety-four that God had forgitten 'im. A toper became a centenarian before "popping his clogs". Pious folk said that strong-drink had killed him.

At Little Rantree, Keasden, lived Dick and his wife, who had been a teacher. She was a nice person and he treated her badly. One day, Dick was mowing with a scythe. He went back home to find his wife dead at the bottom of the stairs. Mrs Swindlehurst was summoned from Bracken Garth to lay her out. That afternoon, he resumed his mowing. Another day, a breathless farmer arrived on Mrs Swindlehurst's doorstep. When he could speak, he said: "Will you come? Our Tom's gone deeard."

John Wallbank, who had a stroke while killing a pig at Mewith Head, lingered for a year and died. It was July, 1914, and some years later a friend said of him: "He missed t'Great War." John had previously requested that his coffin should be transported on a horse-drawn cart, not a hearse. The horse and cart belonged to Matt Hesleton, who dutifully transported the body of John Wallbank to Keasden Church, helped to unload the coffin – then went home.

When Happy Jack died at Keasden, a horse and cart were needed to bear the coffin "up them fields" to the house. To stop it slipping out, a piece of rope was stretched across the back of the cart. Then his friends formed a procession behind the cart as it went down the road to Keasden churchyard. He'd "telled" everyone who would listen that when he died they must bury him "at t'back o' t'dyke" but there wasn't time to consecrate it.

Old Mrs Geldard, of Cappleside, Rathmell, left instructions

that her coffin should be conveyed to the churchyard in a horse-drawn cart belonging to Fred Cornthwaite. "Yon hoss was twenty-eight years old and as stiff as a tree. It could hardly walk." Church folk were enterprising. At one fellside church, the grave was too short for the coffin. So they had the funeral service and left the coffin on the top. A lady member of the congregation changed into old togs, got a spade and clambered into the grave. A man who remained on the surface dug away the extra bit of soil, which fell at the feet of the lady below. She shovelled it out.

Men and women wore crow-black clothes for the funeral. Once the dear-departed had been "putten under", everyone converged on the nearest pub for a meal. A funeral tea involving an aged person tended to be a livelier occasion than a wedding, where everyone was inclined to become weepy. On funeral day, it was concluded that he or she "hed a good life."

Perhaps it was relief at being able to walk out of a graveyard that gave the mourners their high spirits. One mourner, walking down the graveyard path after an interment, said to his companion, a very old chap: "There's not much point in thee going home, is there?"

# PART SIX

# *Dales Encounters*

## KIT CALVERT: THE COMPLETE DALESMAN

My first chat with Kit, half a century ago, was on the bridge spanning Duerley Beck, which was milk-white in its progress down a rock staircase from the fells. Kit, the best-known man in Hawes, removed his battered trilby to reveal grizzle-grey hair that had not been disciplined by a comb. He rekindled his clay pipe with black twist and told me he had tracked down some good "clays" in Northern Ireland. His ragged dog, knowing Kit's propensity for talk, settled down for a nap. In those days, traffic was at ten-minute intervals and, in any case, there would be plenty of time to get out of the way.

Kit pointed to the beckside building where Edward Chapman set up a creamery in 1896, using milk produced on the local farms. When trade slumped in the post-Great War depression, and the closure of the creamery seemed imminent, local farmers found a champion in Kit, who became managing director of a new company, which had a capital of £1,085. In the early 1960s, Kit told me he could not afford to be ill. A new creamery was being built beside the road to Gayle. He must turn up at the site each morning to tell the workmen what to do. I did not dare inquire about planning permission.

Kit loved to talk about the old-style farmhouse Wensleydale cheese, which was softish and mellow. "It more or less melted in the mouth and had a nutty flavour that came from the high moisture content. There was nothing like a good summer-made white Wensleydale. It was one of the casualties of the Second World War. High-moisture cheese didn't fit in with the Ministry of Food's rationing scheme. A good deal of cheese weight might be lost through evaporation. When an individual's ration was an ounce a week this could be irritating to a retailer who received an exact weight of cheese. For this reason, a lot of Wensleydale was sent to a plant for re-processing and distribution among the Armed Services." Only six farmhouse cheese-makers were left in the dale in 1945.

To his regret, it was commercially expedient to change from the cheese's traditional linen bandage and use a polythene wrapping. He introduced the Baby Wensleydale, a one-pound cheese that the average housewife might buy weekly. On one of his rare trips from the Dales, he attended a glittering assembly in Leeds where Wensleydale cheese was being promoted and began his speech with the words: "I'se nobbut a moorbird."

I asked him about whangy cheese. Was it true that you attacked it with an axe? Not quite. It was made out of either blue [skimmed] milk or a blend of skimmed and new. "Some folk were rather greedy. They'd put up the night's milk for butter, take the cream off that milk, and put the skimmed milk into the morning's milk for cheese-making. This cheese didn't get the right amount of butterfat. It was fit for nowt but cooking."

He retired in 1967 when he was sixty-five years old, reputedly with at least half a million pounds in the bank. Wensleydale cheese is still a noted product of Hawes. Every "round pound" that leaves the creamery bears a portrait of Kit, complete with trilby and clay pipe.

Kit Calvert's name survives as that of a bookshop, which is the successor to one he started in 1940 in main street premises he rented from a local solicitor. One of the first incidents he recalled was howling at his father and demanding, of all things, a Collins clear-type dictionary, price one shilling. The howling of this precocious nine-year-old brought results. Father, though a struggling quarryman, bought the book. Kit became a book-collector when he acquired a copy of Edmund Bogg's *Eden Vale to the Plains of York.* "Bogg often came to Hawes, cycling up the dale with a pack of books on his back. He hoped to sell them to the local folk."

Kit paid next-to-nothing for his copy of the rare and handsome *Ogilby's Book of Roads* (1698). He acquired it at a farm sale. "I'd to buy over six hundredweights of books to get this... I didn't bother to bring the others away." Two antiquarian booksellers helped Kit to collect *Mountain Minstrel*, the collected works of Mathew Willis, a local poet. Eventually the volume was found and Kit bought it for ten shillings. Within three months, he saw the local dustman going to the tip with a barrow-load of books. "I offered him a shilling to tip them out and re-load after I had looked through them. My find was another copy of Mathew Willis's book."

When John Mason, an elderly man, helped out at the bookshop after he had clattered round the town in clogs, he placed a card in the window: "Hawes University. Bursar – John Mason." I was with Kit at his home late one afternoon when John, then well into his eighties, arrived somewhat breathlessly with the day's takings – sixpence.

If there was no-one in attendance at the bookshop, a purchaser left any monies in a chapel collection plate. The first honesty box had an anti-theft device. It was nailed to a table. Kit was a Congregational lay preacher who, according to a local poet, F A Carter, "preaches on t'ferst day o' t'week/An' practices on awt' others." During the Second World War he kept a Swaledale chapel open virtually single-handed, motoring over Buttertubs Pass in all weathers.

Kit translated passages of the Bible into the dialect of his native dale so that Jesus, while walking by t'tarnside, and seeing the disciples fishing, shouted: "Copt owt?" To which they replied: "Nowt." Jesus advised them to cast their net on t'other side o' t'boat. When Kit died in 1984, the coffin was borne to its last resting place in Hawes cemetery on a cart drawn by Dolly, his favourite pony. Dolly belonged to his daughter. When she next went riding, Dolly insisted on taking the road to the cemetery. The gate being open, the pony entered and stood near the grave of Thomas Christopher Calvert, who to one and all throughout the northern dales was known simply as Kit.

## FRED LAWSON: ARTIST

Fred, who was born at Yeadon in 1888, visited Castle Bolton, in Wensleydale, on a month's holiday in 1910. He never wanted to leave, having realised an ambition to live by clean streams. "I loved those scraggy bits at the edge of moors where there is water rushing down to the valley."

He tried practically every medium known to the artist, from oil painting to lino cuts, and his favourite was watercolour. While working on a landscape, he preferred to look down into a valley rather than up to the hills. And he walked to his chosen vantage points, observing: "I've found out that people who have cars to carry their stuff do very little painting. They are always looking for something better further along the road. When you're walking, there's a limit as to how far you can go. Then you have to sit down and do something."

Fred had made long jaunts to the Continent but in later life he rarely wandered more than ten miles from home. He was an all-weather painter. On chilly days, he swaddled himself with sacks. In one of the articles he wrote for *The Dalesman*, he noted: "We have had a change today, cool and grey. This morning there was a slight suggestion of a fine drizzle. I went out hoping to get wet, but didn't. This afternoon I went up the ghyll, dull and cool. What a relief after all the heat. They tell me it's a month since we had rain – it seems longer."

When I walked with him on a crisp autumn day in 1955, we left his cottage, at the edge of the village, and had not gone ten yards before he stopped and pointed the stem of his pipe at a building which at one time had been a house. Now the windows were boarded up. "It's a calf-house today," Fred explained, "but Bella Jackson used to live there. She kept six donkeys and went up on to the moor for coal."

We entered a community room that had been a blacksmith's shop. Said Fred: "The last blacksmith was the village tooth-puller as well. He had some little pincers for the job." We passed the old pinfold and stopped where an old donkey hung its head over a fence. It belonged to Walter Bostock, who used it to bring milk from the pastures to the village. This, indeed, was the only donkey left at Castle Bolton. When the villagers owed much of their prosperity to the lead-mines, donkeys were commonly used for transport. After a day's work they were tethered in little plots of land, each about forty yards long by ten yards wide.

Fred's little studio stood half way down the village and was of the one up, one down variety. It was used infrequently. When someone asked him where his studio might be found, he pointed to the window and to the landscape beyond and said: "That's my studio." The busy stem of his pipe flickered in the direction of the road. "Once it was just waterbound and not straight at the edges. They've got a mania now for putting a string down and making everything straight." So we reached the partly-ruined castle. Fred said that at the north-east corner lived an old lady. She kept a pig in the east curtain wall, which was hollow, taking great pains to back it into the narrow space. Not being able to turn round, it would emerge head first in the morning!

Years later, Muriel, his widow, told me more about Fred's love affair with the dale. I remember that afternoon, having called on a stormy day. As dark clouds parted, the gloomy little cottage room was lit up by sunshine in a broad beam, as though from a searchlight. I chose such a moment to photograph her. Fred's sojourn in Wensleydale began after George Graham, artist, paid a short visit and, enchanted, told Fred all about it. Fred joined George on an expedition to the valley. The weather being good, and the days long, they slept in tents but spent most of their daytimes in sketching and painting. They were joined by Jacob Kramer.

Deciding it was practical to make a living as artists in the Dales, Fred and George moved here, George taking rooms in the diminutive *Temperance Hotel*, which then stood at Castle Bolton. Apart from the family, only one guest could be accommodated and, despite the name of the hotel, a barrel of beer was kept for haymakers. Fred found lodgings with Anthony Horner, an old bachelor who made a living from rabbit-catching. Anthony, who had been talking for years about getting married, each evening held a photograph of his lady-love, looked at the print and then put it back where it was being safely kept.

At Carperby, George and Fred had the offer of the lease of what was locally known as Rats' Castle, being no better than its name implied. Fred's parents helped to improve it. Then Bob Horne, who farmed on Lord Bolton's land at Castle Bolton, offered the letting of a detached house. If the two artists would rent the property for a spell, he'd flit them free of charge. They did. He did. Their possessions were moved on a flat horse-drawn cart. Fred told Muriel that he always felt sorry for the horse; it had such a job to get up the hill to the village.

When Muriel first thought of Fred, an older person, in an adult way, he was "slim, very neat and a magnificent swimmer. His hands were small. I was fascinated to see him using them when drawing or painting. He was inspired and not reliant on a set method of painting, as many people are. Fred was very much himself; the lines flowed..." Muriel, the daughter of a Leyburn painter and decorator with the fine old Dales name of Metcalfe, went off to Newcastle to study art. Fred periodically visited her. When her studies were completed, she and Fred worked together at the portrayal of the Dales landscape and people.

His proposal of marriage came one day when he was painting the fair at Leyburn. Muriel recalled: "He loved the colour, movement and excitement of fairgrounds that were held in the dale-country on the old feast days. I sauntered up the town and there he was, just finishing his picture and putting it down carefully so that nobody would trip over it. He had brought out of his pocket his old briar pipe and seemed intent on having a smoke. He leaned against the Town Hall window-cill. I was just eighteen years old but we talked as equals for a minute or two. Fred just looked at me and said: 'Will you marry me?' Just like that. He was absolutely straight. And, of course, I said yes."

The wedding took place in the church at Castle Bolton on a January day a year or two after the proposal. The ceremony was plain, simple and homely. "We went home. George Jackson came in and made a pot of coffee. As we were drinking the coffee a knock came to the door. Fred answered it. The visitors were Harold Thompson and his wife, good friends from Leeds. She said to Fred: "Is this your new housekeeper?" He said: "No – were were married today. This is my wife..."

Fred died in 1968. J B Priestley wrote: "He lived in the Dales; he knew and loved the Dales; and he drew and painted what he saw, year after year, all around him."

# ANNIE MASON: A SCOTTISH CONNECTION

When James Pratt, farmer and cattle dealer of Burtersett, near Hawes, married a daughter of Richard Metcalfe, two well-respected Wensleydale families were united. James was "towards forty years old". Margaret Metcalfe, who was tall and very bonnie, was fifteen years younger. Their daughter, Annie Margaret, heard tales from her of exciting things that had happened in Wensleydale, including the building of the iron railway bridge between Hawes and Askrigg. Mother, as a lile lass, had seen the bridge being built.

Annie sometimes accompanied her father when, each year, he visited Lanark to buy cattle. On one trip she discovered why there should be such a discrepancy in the ages of her parents. They met a well-to-do lady. "James, how are you?" she asked. They held hands. Later, Annie asked her father about the lady he had greeted with such affection. "Oh, she's a very old friend," he replied. Annie commented: "You don't usually hold hands with old friends at home." He said: "Well, you see, I was engaged to that lady and I should have married her."

It seems that father's eldest sister had married a man who unsuccessfully took up farming. In short, he ran out of money, owed large sums to local people and did a "moonlight flit". This was not uncommon except that in his case he "flit" to America. Family honour was a stake. By the time the Pratt family had paid up all the debts in full James, who was then a young man, was left without money. He regretfully gave up his Scottish girl and years later married Miss Metcalfe. It was a happy marriage.

As a young woman, before the Great War, Annie frequently drove the horse-drawn trap from the family farm to t'Junction [Garsdale railway station], taking father to catch an early train to Scotland, where once again he attended the Lanark sales. "We always kept a tight-legged horse for this run." Once, she drove to Garsdale station wearing nothing more than a nightdress, with a coat thrown over it. They had been late astir and it was a rush to catch the train. As she returned through Appersett, an old lady came out of her house and offered a warming cup of tea. James was such a good customer of the Midland Railway that when he missed the train by a minute or two, Mr Bunce the stationmaster allowed him to ride on the pilot engine and board the train at Appleby.

In a few days following James Pratt's departure, cattle began to arrive at Garsdale by rail. Unloaded from special wagons, they were driven on foot to Burtersett and the fell-side grazings. "Sometimes, at Garsdale, the railwaymen would shunt a bit roughly. One of our cows had a hip out. Father always had a law suit going with the railway company for one thing or another."

When Annie was seventeen years, and once again visiting Lanark with her father, they were intrigued by the unusual bustle at the *Caledonian Hotel.* What great event was going to take place? The manager approached James Pratt and announced it was in his honour. "You have stayed with us each year for sixty years." Said James, to his daughter: "It's nowt to get bothered about." Yet at heart he appreciated the gesture, especially as the directors of the hotel company came down from Glasgow and "we had a very nice meal."

It was the twilight of the droving days, during which large numbers of Highland cattle on foot had been driven along ancient rights of way, to be fattened up on the rich pastures of the Dales before being sold for consumption by families in the fast-developing industrialised towns of the North. Annie remembered taking a drover from Wensleydale to Alston, here to collect from a Scottish drover the cattle that an Englishman would now attend.

The Pratts of Burtersett had the first mowing machine in the district. Village folk shook their heads when they saw it operating. They dolefully forecast that the fog [second flush of grass] would never grow. As a child, Annie Mason was allowed to go round with a bell that was rung for the start of Hawes Fair, held in late September. "They had the 'coming-in day' when people brought their stock. There were stalls at the bottom end of the town, below the post office. The Market Hall at Hawes was the place where you sold your butter and eggs. 'It's actually the Market House'."

It was James Pratt, along with T T Iveson, who started the auction mart at Hawes in 1885. James had sold cattle and sheep in the open street times without number. It was the period when sovereigns were exchanged and there was a firm hand-clasp to seal a bargain. James felt that Hawes and Hellifield, having good rail connections, were first-rate places for stock-trading.

In the back-end of the year, James Pratt bought some sheep in Scotland. They were pure Scotlanders, as the Pratt family called them. Annie recalled: "Up to the slopes of Wether Fell they went. We got overstocked with sheep in those days and so they sent some for wintering to Brimham Rocks, above Nidderdale. I remember one winter when there was a big snow as they were due to come back." Other farmers' sheep were also to be returned to the home farms. The journey of the Pratts' stock would take several days. "When they had been two or three days coming, I was sent up to beyond Gayle on horseback with two bundles of hay, one on each side of the horse. I would use this hay to 'tice [entice] the sheep down. I also had some provisions – ham sandwiches and various things – for the men to eat."

Annie's mother had been to Liverpool and she had bought a thermos flask, the first to be seen in the upper dale. "She made some coffee, put some rum in it and poured it into the thermos flask. I will always remember going up to old Dick Fawcett and asking him if he would like a drop of coffee. He put the thermos to his lips and, of course, it was full of hot coffee. 'What the devil's in this?' he shouted." It was vital to keep the sheep walking – hence the use of hay. Over Fleet Moss from Langstrothdale came animals belonging to the Pratts and the Fawcetts, each sheep treading in the footsteps of the one that had gone before. "We had no trouble shedding-off Mr Fawcett's sheep. When they came to his open gate, they 'shed' themselves off. I got to the bottom of the hill and looked back. I could see a dark line of sheep all the way down the slope."

Annie Pratt became Mrs Mason and, like her father, a much-respected member of the dale community.

## JOSSIE ATKINSON: FELL FARMER

Jossie was "at home" in the sense that he was on his fell-side farm in Mallerstang. Now eighty-six years old and with a "pot" foot, Jossie had lived alone for years. I parked my car at the side of the dale road, crossed a field, then a bridge over the river. There was another field, then a third, this one rising steeply to where Cumpstone Hill farm stood near the old highway used by Lady Anne Clifford twixt her relations at Nappa Hall, Wensleydale, and her castle of Pendragon.

I rapped on the main door of Cumpstone Hill. There was no reply. I went through this routine three times and meanwhile made local inquiries about Jossie. As I climbed to the farm yet again, I saw him, slowly returning from a spell of gap-walling. As a waller, he was a dale celebrity. Local farmers talked about the six-week spell during which he erected 170 yards of wall. "That was a fair do for a man as old as me... I don't like to do a lot o' walking; my pot leg gets gey tired."

Jossie moved to the farm in 1930, which was not a good

time. "Some o' t'land has gone back and some is better than it was." He recalled when hired shepherds tended the flocks on gaited pastures [a gait relates to the pasturage needed by a single sheep]. He had memories of trudging round the fells in hot weather, looking for maggoty sheep. In t'owd days, farmers were forever looking at their sheep. "They could nearly allus find summat wrang."

Inside his kitchen-cum-living room I saw the basic elements of the old Dales house – fireplace incorporating oven and boiler, burning peat and a lile bit of coal; a flagged floor with pegged rug, rocking chair and a large deal table. Jossie "fetched" peat from the moor with a coup cart [box-type sled hauled by a horse]. Peats were grand on baking day; they were terribly hot. "If there was a lile bit o' red in t'bottom of your fire, and you broke a peat up, it started off practically right away."

Jossie used to go to a fell-end pit in Cotterdale [just over the hill] for coal. "Bogeys ran in and out o' t'mine. Each bogey held eight hundredweight, for which a farmer paid about 3s.6d. Cotterdale coal, being small, was poured on to a hot peat fire and allowed to cake. Then you had to stab it wi' t'poker." We stared at the fireplace. A curl of blue-grey smoke rose up the chimney. Jossie said it had not been cleaned out for years. He used to climb on the house-roof and drop down the chimney a sled rope weighted by a stone. He then tied on the rope a sack filled with bedding. When the bottom of the chimney had been blocked off, the sack was pulled up and down a number of times, displacing the soot.

He had used the oven for all kinds of jobs. Pigs used to be big and very fat. "I killed a pig when t'last war was on and, using yon oven, I rendered down twenty-eight pound o' fat. By gum, it came in useful did that. You were rationed for lard and, being a fat pig, when you fried owt you could get a potful oot o' t'frying pan. Fat was worth more than t'bacon to owd folk. Long sen it was all dipping into t'frying pan wi' slices o' bread. There's nowt o' that now."

I pointed to a cupboard set in the wall near the fireplace. Had he kept his salt there so it would remain dry? "We kept all sorts o' things, maybe bottles of cow medicine. I used to doctor mi own stock. If I'd a cow that calved and it didn't 'clean' within five or six hours, I'd wait till it had been calved 24 hours and then get a pint o' cream and a tablespoonful o' salt petre. I'd mix it in cream and give it to t'cow in a horn, t'sort we used for dosing. In an hour or two you'd see t'cleansing come. If it didn't shift it, you had to give it another dose, twelve hours later. But it nearly always worked t'first time." (Years later, I passed this tip on to a farmer with a cow in the same circumstances; it worked!).

If Jossie had a sheep that was having difficulties a-lambing, he used his lambing oil – a tablespoonful of turpentine and a tablespoonful of watter in a little bottle. "If I had my hand to put into that sheep to git that lamb, I'd git this bottle out and give her that at her mouth. I never had one that festered."

Jossie had a wireless. He had noted the many serious road accidents being reported. He smiled, then said: "I think I'se safer hoppin' about up here!"

## SIR RUPERT HART-DAVIS: PUBLISHER

He first set eyes on the Dales in 1947, when David Garnett, an old friend and colleague, lent him a cottage at Butt's Intake on Whitaside from which he had a splendid view of Swaledale. The cottage had been advertised in *The Lady* and was rented from an old lady for £5 a year. It was his holiday home for years. "David thought that Swaledale was the most beautiful place he had ever seen; so did I, the moment I got there." Sir Rupert was still living in the valley of the Swale when I called to see him in 1985. I apologise for calling unannounced. It seems that this was the best chance of meeting him. He no longer made appointments.

For thirty-five years, Rupert Hart-Davis was a much-respected London publisher. In his old age, he cherished the quietness of his book-lined study in the Old Rectory at Marske. "I always wanted to live in a beautiful place and read and write books. Now I am doing it. My dream has come true..." His collection of books was moved from London to Swaledale in 169 tea chests.

Just after the 1939-45 war, in which he saw military service, holidays spent in Swaledale were a tonic for mind and body. The war had little effect on Dales life. "Most of the people had not been disturbed much. No bombs had fallen anywhere near. The only complaints I heard in the late 1940s was a shortage of cigarettes." Rationing was still officially in force but the local grocer always gave them a little extra butter and sugar. "We were in-comers and strangers but he was extremely good to us."

The cottage on Whitaside had two names – Butt's Intake and Duke Mary's. The last name related to Mary Duke, a former resident. Reaching the cottage from London demanded an eight-hour drive. For a time, the Hart-Davis family rented, for holidays, a cottage at Thwaite. Then they discovered a ruined cottage high on Kisdon hill, overlooking Keld. "It had one room up, one room down and a sort of hutch off it. And it had been empty for fifty years. There were about eighteen inches of sheep droppings, upstairs as well as downstairs."

Percy Calvert, the builder, tapped the floor, walls and roof and said: "It's all sound. I'll fettle it up for you." The lessee said: "Well, you've got to get this stuff off the floor, you know." Percy replied: "Oh, we'll have to get a woman to do that." Two poor old ladies from Keld came up and cleared all the mess away."

The hilltop cottage had no electricity, no water and no

drainage. "I managed to buy it after a tremendous tussle with Willie Whitehead, who lived at Pry House. The main snag was that two fields went with it. I didn't want the two fields. Eventually I bought it from him for £250, which then was quite a lot of money. Percy Calvert and his splendid men put it in order for us. We used it for holidays from 1955 until 1964, when we moved to Marske."

In correspondence with a former schoolmaster at Eton, Rupert penned a goodly number of letters from the cottage on Kisdon in the late spring, when they spent much time here. He mentioned events in his simple and down-to-earth Dales life – looking for bird nests, enjoying walks and admiring the spectacle of a profuse and varied flora. He attended a village sale and spent 21s.6d on a looking glass for the bedroom. Standing outside the cottage at night, he saw only four lights strung along the bottom of the valley; three in farmhouses and the fourth in the telephone box in Keld. "It is on all night and doubtless we all pay for it."

For years, the Hart-Davis's had to climb over a six-foot wall and go to a water trough for their supply. So they had a piped water supply installed. "It was a plastic pipe, fed by a spring further up the hill and directed into the back of the house, within which a sink and tap were fitted." Rupert had always intended to retire to Swaledale but a cottage at the top of a hill was not a place for a person to spend his old age. It couldn't be reached except with a Land Rover. "Otherwise you had to walk up, which took twenty minutes, with rests, and you spent rather less time walking down."

He was driving to Richmond on the top road when he saw an empty house at Marske. It had been the Rectory and belonged to the Church."I went to the post office and inquired about it. They let me have the key. My wife and I went over it and thought it was marvellous, though it was in a terrible state. Cows had got in downstairs and it was full of dead birds and prayer books and soot and things. Dirty. Horrible."

The house and front field were coming up for auction. "My wife had flu and must stay in London so I came up to the auction, which was at the *King's Head* in Richmond. One man bid against me. I got it for £4,200 and felt that if that man had not been there I would have been able to buy it for almost half the price because nobody else was bidding." Years afterwards, a man rang the door bell and announced that he was the chap who had bid against him. Could he look round the house? "Yes, of course." Rupert asked him if he had intended to knock the house down and make it into flats or live in it. He said he had intended to live there.

The field at the back was purchased from the Church authority. "They said that before it could be sold, I would have to get a faculty to de-consecrate the path from the gate to the new churchyard. I wrote back and said 'there is no path and there never has been a path; it's a green field.' They then wrote and said I needed another faculty to enable me to step over this path. I signed an enormous document. One clause said that no chickens would be allowed to run in this field. So I said to them I had not intention of running chickens, but why not? Oh, was the reply, they might fly into the churchyard and dig up the graves. Can you imagine such a circumstance? It took me six months to get them to sell it."

The restoration was costly, as it might be with a house of twenty-three rooms. It had been built in 1753 and was extended about 1850 when the parson took in pupils. "We have a garden in front, a rose garden down the road and an acre by the beck at the bottom... A friend who came to tea said: 'You know, if you are living in this beautiful place and doing the things you want to do, you are half-way to heaven." In his old age, his dream of a reflective retirement in which he might read and write had come true.

# Further reading in the W.R. Mitchell range of books

## 'Summat & Nowt - Memories of a Yorkshire Editor'

A light-hearted review of his 50 years' association with The Dalesman magazine, the oldest and most popular of Yorkshire magazines. Bill's many years of writing about the Dales, which included articles each month following handing over editorship in 1988, gave him a wealth of stories and information of his travels throughout the region meeting Dalesfolk in every corner of this special part of Yorkshire.

**168 pages with illustrations by Richard Bancroft - £9.95**

## 'Nobbut Middlin' - Laugh with the Dalesfolk'

The third book written by W. R. 'Bill' Mitchell in a trilogy of humorous ccounts from Dalesfolk. The intension is to amuse and also to evoke life as it was in the Yorkshire ales. The author, who edited The Dalesman maga-ine for many years, has witnessed the transforma-tion of an insular, self-reliant way of life into one in which Dales farming as we have known it is struggling to survive.

**128 pages with colour photographs and illustrations - £9.95**

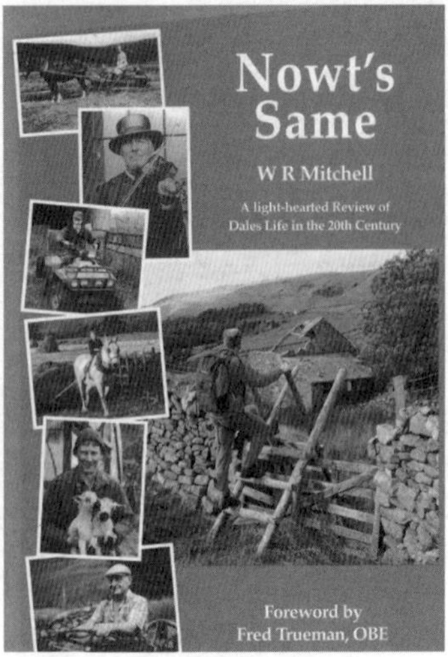


## 'Nowt's Same - A Light-hearted review of Dales Life in the 20th Century'

Dales life is recalled through folks tales and mu humour. In 1900, women showed little more than ankles to the gaze of the opposite sex. A prudish Dales housewife covered the bare legs the living room table on Sundays. Ninety-nine ye later, members of the Rylstone Women's institute able to raise money for charity by posing unclad, calendar. In Grandma's day, chests were rubbed v goose grease and working-class folk were often 'right pickle'.

**136 pages with illustrations by Richard Bancroft - £9.95**

## 'Yorkshire Dalesfolk' - Yesterday and Today'

Within its nine chapters, this fully illustrated paperback covers life in the Dales over the years. With fascinating and rare photographs, the author looks at -

**T'Owd Days**
**Farm Folk**
**Hay Crop**
**Stone Walling**
**Horses and Ponies**
**Sheep Dogs**
**Native Sheep**
**Settle- Carlisle Railway Connections**
**Celebrities**

**40 pages with colour and black and white photographs - £7.95**

Watershed Mill, Settle, North Yorkshire BD24 9LR
www.railwayvideo.com